modern astrology

MODERN
astrology

Harness the Stars to Discover Your Soul's True Purpose

LOUISE EDINGTON

ALTHEA
PRESS

Interior Designer: Lauren Smith
Cover Designer: Will Mack and Emma Hall
Editor: Nana K. Twumasi
Production Editor: Erum Khan

Author photo © Don Hajicek, 2018

ISBN: Print 978-1-64152-226-7 | eBook 978-1-64152-227-4

For Maridel Bowes, without whom I would not be the Astrologer I am, and for Charles, Molly and Alice, without whom I would not be the person I am today.

contents

introduction

AFTER NEARLY 30 YEARS of study and practice, I know firsthand how powerful astrology can be as a tool for personal growth. I have always been interested in how the planets affect us; I still have childish scribbles that I wrote as a young girl about the Sun signs, and I have always looked up at the sky in wonderment.

At my first Saturn return in 1989 at the age of 29—a time of profound significance in astrology—a friend read my natal chart and taught me how to calculate charts in the days before personal computers were common. I was hooked. At that time, charts were hand drawn and calculated using tables of values, requiring an ephemeris, a *Tables of Houses* reference guide, and a book of time zones. It was a lengthy process that took about an hour and a half. These were useful tools for helping understand the makeup of the chart. Fortunately for modern astrologers, today this process takes minutes using computer programs and printers.

For many years, I studied books on astrology and practiced working with my chart and the charts of friends and their children. My chart interpretations were always accurate, even with my self-taught and unintegrated interpretation. I had not yet learned to see the natal chart as a whole. My first interpretations were much like the printed software interpretations that anyone can now access if they have astrological software, reports explaining that the Sun in Virgo means one thing, the Moon in Leo means another, and so on. My early interpretations took no account of aspects or house placements. There is some value in these simple interpretations, but they don't look at the chart as a whole, which is what this book encourages you to do.

In 2012, I made the decision to begin practicing astrology as a career and undertook more formal training. This is when I discovered Evolutionary Astrology (also known as Soul Astrology). Evolutionary Astrology involves more of a psychological or counseling approach to astrology. It is perfectly suited for inspiring personal-development goals. Evolutionary Astrology is the "school" of astrology I speak about in this book as I guide you to look at each area of your chart as an opportunity for growth, based on a deep self-knowledge rather than on generic tools that apply to everyone. Personally, Evolutionary Astrology has helped me reach a place of deep contentment, acceptance, and happiness.

When used appropriately, astrology is one of the best tools for personal development. When you are born, a cosmic blueprint of your soul's evolution in this lifetime is created based on the date, time, and place of your birth. Evolutionary Astrology posits that your soul chose the time, date, and place of your birth so that you are given the opportunity to fulfill an evolutionary purpose from karmic lessons (a spiritual principle of cause and effect) from previous lifetimes. You are born with a persona (public image or personality, as distinguished from the inner self), ego (the part of you that mediates between the conscious and the unconscious), and soul (the spiritual or immaterial part of you that is regarded as immortal), which is designed to fulfill an evolutionary purpose. Your chart provides the map to help you discover and fulfill that purpose.

Armed with this self-knowledge and acceptance, you can navigate personal issues and problems in alignment with how you work best. The aim of this book, therefore, is not to teach you how to be an astrologer; it is to teach you how to use astrology as a tool to help you along your life's path.

Your natal chart is a blueprint that evolves over your lifetime based on how you respond and react to outer events and the evolutionary spiral of unfolding that planetary transits bring. You always have free will and choice in every single moment of your life. You choose how you embody the energies in the natal chart since all placements have both "higher" and "lower" vibrations. You also choose how you respond and react to the evolutionary planetary cycles throughout your life and how they impact your natal chart. Your soul chooses a general path of evolutionary development, but throughout life, you possess free will to choose which direction to go in and which traits to consciously activate. This book asks you to get to know the traits, or energies, in your natal chart at a deep level so that you can choose consciously and with awareness.

Your current life is shaped by your past lives, and your soul desires to learn from that past. For example, in a previous lifetime, you may have been a powerful person who exercised power in an unhealthy way over others; in this lifetime, your lesson will be how to use power in a right and just way.

You can always choose the way you respond to the cosmic blueprint (your natal chart) that you were born with and how you respond to the evolutionary triggers in the spiral of your soul's growth. It is the awareness and consciousness of the energies in your chart that help you better make choices that bring you closer to your soul's desire and evolutionary purpose.

In your natal chart, you have the planets, the luminaries (Sun and Moon, grouped with the planets), and points such as the Moon's Nodes that indicate the "what" in your chart. The Sun is your core or ego, the Moon is your emotional body, Pluto is your soul's desire, and so on—you'll learn more in the upcoming chapters. The 12 zodiac signs are "how" these luminaries express themselves in this lifetime, and the 12 houses are the areas of life where those particular bodies are most impactful.

Your natal chart also takes into account the angles (the cusps of the first, seventh, tenth, and fourth houses), which include the Ascendant (your persona; how people see you when they first meet you one-on-one); Midheaven (your mission); Descendant (the "other" in your life, as well as relationships and the disowned self, or rejected parts of the self you may feel are socially unacceptable); and the Nadir or Imum Coeli (your inner life). All of this provides a complex blueprint of the self in this lifetime.

It takes time and study to be able to read this complex blueprint on behalf of others. It *is* possible, however, to look at your own blueprint to gain a deep understanding and acceptance of who you are and how you work. There is a lot of information here and in your chart, so take it one step at a time. The more you study and explore your chart, the more it will all begin to make sense.

Personal growth or development is not about becoming something you are not; it is not about fixing anything or dwelling on perceived flaws. You are who you are. The astrology of personal development brings awareness and choice with regard to how you embody the energies in your chart. Your emotional body is whatever it is according to sign, house, and aspects. Knowledge of this enables you to become more aware of your emotional reactivity, and that in itself lessens the intensity of it. In other words, you are able to take a slight step back and acknowledge your reactions and make a more conscious choice. There are *always* choices.

Throughout this book, I show you how you can make choices within each area of your chart. No choice is better or worse than the other—it is just a choice. Having this knowledge means that you are choosing with awareness rather than floating through life at the whim of the cosmic energies and your blueprint. My wish for you is that this book guides you along your journey to learn more about yourself, promote your personal growth, and find deep self-acceptance and happiness.

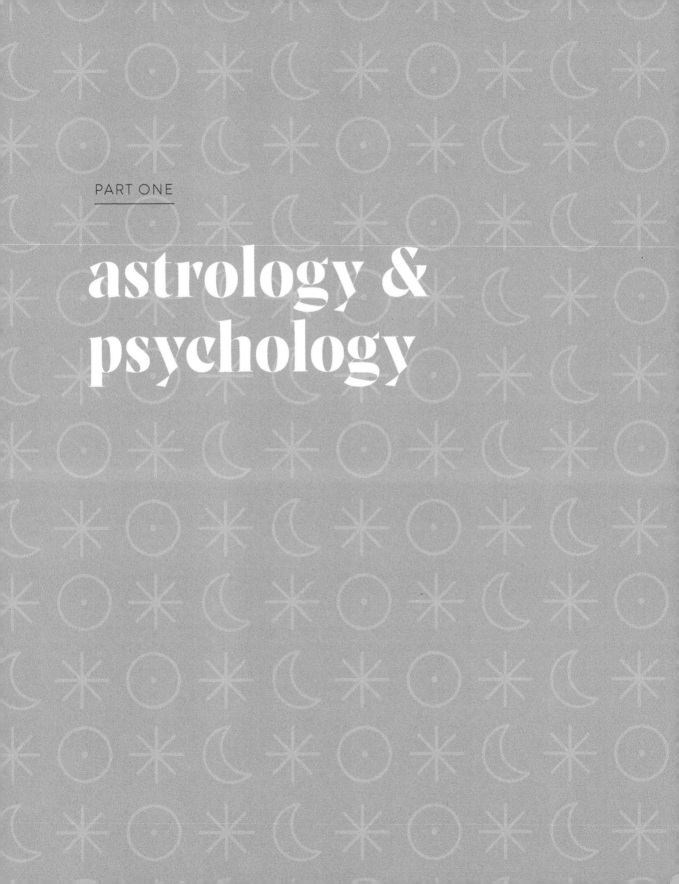

astrology & psychology

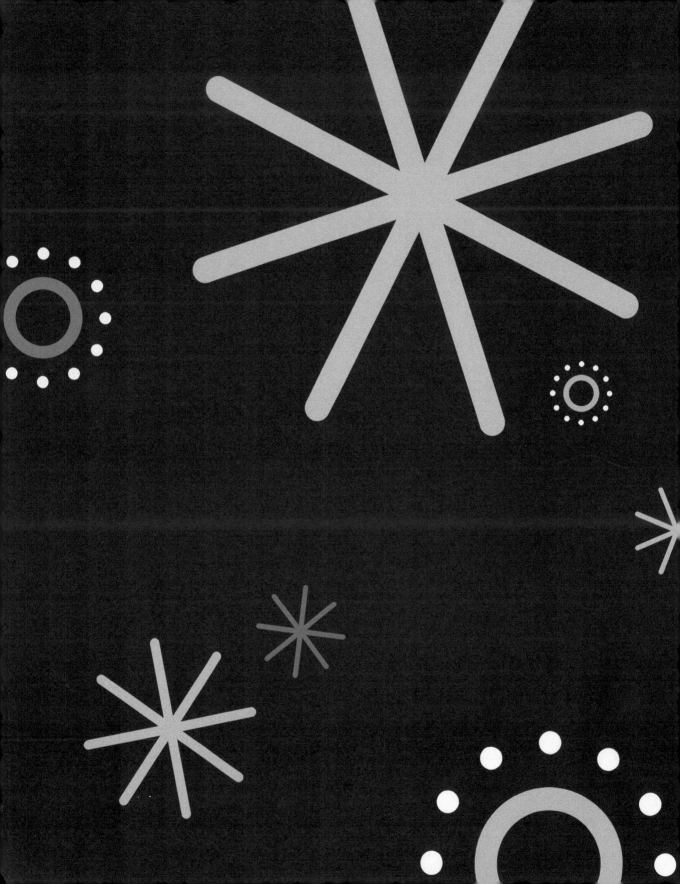

interpreting the stars as tools for growth

Astrology is assured of recognition from psychology, without further restrictions, because astrology represents the summation of all the psychological knowledge of antiquity.
—CARL JUNG

Astrology has been used for centuries to give people a clearer sense of who they are and what they need out of life, but much of the available information in the past amounted to general descriptions of personalities, as if they were set in stone with no room for change. Predictive astrology was used to look at the future, but because there are so many variables, predictions were often wrong. That's not to suggest that there are not some excellent "mundane astrologers"— that is, astrologers who predict worldly events, such as times of challenge in economics and politics. That, however, is not what most people are interested in when they turn to astrology to learn something deeper about themselves.

WATCHING THE STARS

For millennia, humans have gazed up to the stars and recognized the connection between the cosmic cycles and movement of the heavens as having an effect on earth. For example, the seasons and tides are clearly affected by cosmic cycles. At some point, they came to understand that cosmic cycles also have an effect on us. In fact, astrology, in one form or another, has been around for thousands of years as a divinatory tool used to predict global and personal events. There is some evidence that the ancient Sumerians used the cosmos as a guide. The Babylonians are generally credited with creating the first organized system of astrology, but there is no specific evidence of the organization they used.

Natal or horoscopic astrology is thought to have begun around 4300 BCE with the ancient Egyptians, who used astrology to look at a person's character based on their date of birth. The Chinese developed a system of astrology around 2800 BCE, and the Greeks melded Egyptian astrology with what they learned from the Babylonians. Around 50 CE, Ptolemy, a Greco-Roman mathematician, astronomer, and astrologer, wrote a book called *Tetrabiblos*. This work originated the current practice of using planets, houses, and signs. After the fall of Rome in 476 CE, astrology began to decline in popularity. It experienced a brief revival during the Renaissance, then fizzled out again until the beginning of the twentieth century, with the birth of the psychological approach to astrology.

Dane Rudhyar was one of the forerunners of this modern movement with the publication of his 1936 book *The Astrology of Personality*. Rudhyar studied astrology and the writings of the Swiss psychiatrist Carl Jung, and he began to synthesize the two. For Rudhyar, this synthesis overcame the deterministic, fated approach of astrology. Put simply, Rudhyar saw the heavens as synchronistically aligned to people. Interestingly, this major shift aligns with the discovery of Pluto in 1930, which is still deemed important by astrologers, despite being recently demoted to being a dwarf planet by astronomers. Pluto's themes of death, rebirth, the shadow, and the soul, are very much in alignment with the therapeutic approach to astrology.

Much of modern Western astrology takes a psychological, counseling based, and evolutionary approach to help seekers understand themselves at a deeper level, guiding them through life's rough spots and helping them see the evolutionary potential of their souls in this lifetime. Since the birth of the New Age movement in the 1960s and 1970s, astrology grew exponentially in popularity. Though much modern astrology takes the psychological approach, there is also a revival of older models and uses for astrology such as the Hellenistic model, which was practiced primarily in the areas surrounding the Mediterranean from approximately the first century BCE until the seventh century CE. The Hellenistic model uses the traditional planets and rulerships but does not include the more recently discovered planets: Uranus, Neptune, and Pluto.

The cosmos is based on cycles and circles. The movement of all atomic structures on earth is mirrored in the movements of the planets in our galaxy and in the movement of the galaxy within the universe, moving as spirals within spirals, and so it is within us. Aligning with the planetary phases and rhythms brings flow to our lives as we evolve with the cosmic energies rather than fight against them. With this knowledge, you are able to face challenging energies with a more philosophical approach as you begin to embody the flow and cyclical nature of life, the earth, and the universe, knowing that all is evolving as you are.

I invite you, alongside your reading of this book, absorbing the astrological language, and practicing the exercises in the chapters, to actually get outside and look up. Technology has given us amazing resources, such as apps like Star Walk and Sky Guide, to aid in identifying planetary bodies and helping you witness and *feel* the cyclical nature of the whole universe. This will help you embrace the energies and even the challenging times, knowing that growth is within the grasp of your whole being. Tune in to both your inner world and the movement of the universe so that you can move toward your soul's evolutionary potential with relative ease and grace.

ASTROLOGY: A PSYCHOLOGICAL APPROACH

A general practice of astrology can make it seem like we are at the whim of fate and the planetary movements of the cosmos, while *psychological* astrology, or Evolutionary Astrology, shows us that the choices we make direct the course of our lives, and that astrology can be used as a functional tool for deepening our knowledge of ourselves. This approach to astrology looks at you as a whole person with an individual soul path and purpose that both follows and utilizes the cycles, positions, and interrelationships contained within the universe.

Jung himself used astrology with his patients. Speaking of the melding of astrology and psychology, he said, "The starry vault of heaven is in truth the open book of cosmic projection, in which are reflected the mythologems, i.e., the archetypes. In this vision astrology and alchemy, the two classical functionaries of the psychology of the collective unconscious, join hands." It's a huge and deep topic, but to try to put it simply: Psychological astrology uses many of the themes developed primarily by Jung, such as archetypes, synchronicity, the shadow, the collective unconscious, and the persona (see the sidebar on page 8). You will explore such concepts in the discussions throughout this book.

As a therapeutic tool, astrology is continually developing, evidenced by the work of astrologers like Liz Greene, Stephen Arroyo, Richard Tarnas, and more. The information in this book is designed to be more accessible to you than a text written specifically for astrologers, but you are free to expand your investigation into more in-depth resources. See page 223 for a list of further reading.

Today, astrology is experiencing a resurgence. I could explain the astrological basis for this resurgence, but that would be a whole book in itself. Much of it has to do with the precession of the zodiac and that we are moving into the Age of Aquarius, which is considered a period of human awakening in astrology. We are in a time of major shifts and changes, and people are seeking answers and guidance to manage the collective changes we are going through.

Astrology is a valuable tool for helping us make sense of the shifts and changes and to move to a place of realization that change comes from within. Additionally, astrology is so much more accessible these days with the development of programs and apps that can help you "read" your natal chart without the help of an astrologer. There are also so many astrologers giving excellent, life-enhancing advice on the Internet.

Applying astrology to everyday life is useful in many areas. As a tool for personal development, the study of astrology offers rapid understanding of the self at a soul level and can circumvent the need for a long journey of self-exploration. Your entire soul is laid bare in your natal chart, alongside your soul's desires and evolutionary impulses. It could be said that astrology can be a fast track to self-knowledge, personal growth, and guidance through the ups and downs of life.

The aim of using astrology for your own personal growth is to get to know and understand the planetary energies and cycles so well that you can learn to *embody* the energies in your natal chart with awareness and thereby use your free will to create your life consciously.

PERSONAL DEVELOPMENT

Through a deep understanding and acceptance of the self and how we work best as individuals, we are able to break unhealthy patterns and habits, understand how we respond and react to external stimuli, and develop healthy ways of interacting with the world based on our soul's unique map. We are able to stop trying to be like others. We can understand and follow our passions and purpose. This helps rid us of the "shoulds" of life: "You should do things this way" runs your thoughts no more.

Astrology helps us rationalize and navigate challenging times, and even helps predict when those periods are coming rather than being thrown around by the cosmic energies.

RELATIONSHIPS AND RELATING TO OTHERS

Basic knowledge of astrology not only helps with self-knowledge, but it also shows how you relate to others in your life. This can be used to understand others at a deeper level, and help you relate with that deeper level of understanding. For example, if you have Taurus Ascendant, you may find yourself continually drawn to people with strong Scorpio energy (the sign on the seventh house cusp), which brings deep compassion and meaning into your life, but then Scorpio's tendency to create conflict can also bring difficulties into your relationships at times. Rather than retreat from the relationship by default, your awareness of this tendency within the energy you are attracted to can enable you to voice your concerns and ask how you can manage this together to create balance. Or you may become aware that you are overly focused on the material side of the relationship and choose to shift your focus to the deeper emotional bond.

ACHIEVING GOALS

Astrology can help you identify and move toward your life goals. Goals are all well and good, but all too often, we look outside of ourselves to identify them. Wouldn't it be more fulfilling to base your goals on how you work best and what your soul really desires? If you are a Sagittarius, for example, fixed goals will rarely work for you; your goals work best with a flexible, bigger-picture element.

Archetypes, Synchronicity, the Shadow, the Collective Unconscious, and the Persona

The following is a simplified explanation of some huge principles to provide you with basic knowledge as you move through this book. If you wish to explore these principles in greater depth, turn to page 223 for further reading.

Archetypes

Archetypes are models into which human personality traits tend to group. In psychological astrology, these traits are generally connected to archetypes recognized by Jung and are attributed to the 12 signs as 12 different characters, sort of like roles in a play. For example, Aries is the warrior; Taurus is the creator, and so on.

Synchronicity

According to Jung, "Synchronicity is the coming together of inner and outer events in a way that cannot be explained by cause and effect and that is meaningful to the observer." Again, this is a vast topic, but, in astrology, this suggests that there is a synchronistic relationship between the universe and human consciousness that is meaningful and cannot be explained by cause and effect. In other words, the universe and humanity are in sync.

The Shadow

The shadow refers to a rejected or unconscious part of the personality that is seen as or felt to be undesirable for any number of societal or psychological reasons such as anger, greed, or selfishness. In astrology, this generally refers to the more negative traits of each sign that we do not like in ourselves.

Collective Unconscious

According to Jung, the collective unconscious is populated by shared instincts and archetypal patterns that underpin how humans instinctively act; this is separate from our individual unconscious. In astrology, this is used to describe unconscious motivations that are not ascribed to our own personal experience.

Persona

Persona refers to the outer part of the personality and is used to describe that which others see of us, usually the Ascendant (see page 18).

To see where this could become a problem, it would also be useful to tap into the detail energy of the opposite sign, Gemini, to help you identify some goals that are achievable in the short term so that you are not always missing the aligned action.

CAREERS

I began my professional career in astrology by doing short career reports for teens, and they were life-changing and deeply meaningful for those young people. Because of the emphasis on self-knowledge in astrology for personal growth, this self-knowledge can help you identify career paths that fit you, rather than trying to fit into an unsuitable career path.

When identifying career possibilities in the chart, note that the chart doesn't identify one career path. The chart identifies the *type* of work you are suited to, and also the environment in which you may find fulfillment.

The chart can also can identify more general career themes, such as whether work that keeps you on the move is best for you, or whether working from a home office might be more suited to your personality. For example, someone with a Sagittarius Midheaven (the cusp of the tenth house, which is the most pubic point in the chart) will be drawn to careers that involve some kind of teaching or counseling. The ruler of Sagittarius, Jupiter, is in the eighth house in Scorpio, which would mean this person may be drawn to either teaching deep psychological principles or having a counseling practice that deals with the shadow. This person may have Leo on the cusp, which means they would need recognition for their work. (Please note that these are examples and not the only possibilities.)

The words and phrases I use throughout this book and in Appendix B help you identify the energy of each sign or planet, but they are only suggestions. If you would like, you can look up synonyms, or think of similar words and phrases that better resonate with you. Jot them down in a journal.

You now have a brief history of astrology and a basic understanding of how astrology for personal growth developed. This chapter introduced you to how astrology can be used by you to better understand and approach your soul's journey.

I hope you now have your natal chart in hand. If you are unfamiliar with these charts, it might look somewhat confusing to you, but in the next chapter, you will find an overview of the natal chart and what is contained within it so that you can better understand what you are looking at. This will give you the tools you need to use the rest of the book.

Natal Chart Resources

To get the most out of this book, you will need to have your natal chart in hand and be able to identify your Sun sign, rising sign (Ascendant), and where the planets are in your chart. If you aren't able to have your chart professionally done before using this book (the most recommended approach), there are a few online resources to draw up your own chart.

You will need to provide the date, time, and place of birth, which can be found on some birth certificates or by asking parents and relatives. An accurate time of birth is necessary to calculate the house positions and angles in the chart. If it turns out that your chart does not resonate with you, double-check the time of your birth. If you don't know the time, you can still glean a lot of information from the signs the planets are in, but you would not want to pay attention to the houses and angles. However, if you know approximately what time you were born, your Moon placement will be fairly accurate.

TimePassages by Astrograph.com has both Windows and iOS software, and an iOS app. The levels range from a free basic version to paid options.

Astro Gold is available as an app for Android and iOS devices, and as software for macOS (OSX) 10.8 or higher, for a fee. Astro Gold is adding to its capabilities constantly.

Astro.com is one of the most widely used resources, and it is free, but it is not necessarily the easiest to navigate. It does give many more options than other free sites, however.

your natal chart, yourself

As above, so below; as within, so without. —HERMES TRISMEGISTUS

The natal chart is a cosmic blueprint of the soul's incarnation in this lifetime. It shows traits, possibilities, soul lessons, the soul's evolutionary purpose, and more. Contained within that blueprint is you, as reflected in the cosmos. In this chapter, we'll take a look at the individual parts of the chart and what they each mean. If you are familiar with astrology, this chapter will be a refresher for you. If not, then it will give you the basics to begin understanding your own chart.

THE NATAL CHART: AN OVERVIEW

I have included a sample natal chart on page 15 for you to refer to as I move through different elements of the chart. I offer some specific examples in the following discussions of how the energies show themselves, but I cover more specifics later for each sign so there's no need to commit the examples I use to memory.

Keep in mind that your chart will look different, but the basic elements will be the same. I will not take you through every single detail of the chart because that can become overwhelming. Instead, I will take you through the particular aspects that will help you get a deeper self-understanding, and I will provide tools to help you integrate and navigate what you learn.

This book specifically looks at the planets and houses in each sign. It will not look at the planets in each house, but, using the tools provided, you will be able to interpret those yourself. This book also teaches about aspects and transits (especially in chapter 15), but it does not delineate them individually.

Later, you will learn about the energies of each sign, the planets in each sign, and the signs in the houses. But first, you will need to identify the symbols and elements in your chart. The sample chart is labeled to help you on your way. For a quick review of the symbols and glyphs associated with the planets and signs, you can turn to the glossary on page 220; they are also included with each discussion.

THE SUN ☉

The Sun is our very core or ego; it is both the central organizing principle of the galaxy and our self. Much of our personality is predicated on our Sun sign, which is why the horoscopes you might read online or in periodicals are generally based on Sun signs. It's also the easiest to identify because it is based only on your birthdate. The Sun is how we most often identify as the Self. It is often seen as the "male" or "father" energy in the chart. It's our being and our becoming, what our innate character is, and who we are learning to be in this lifetime. The Sun in your chart represents life, heart, vitality, essence, and consciousness.

The sign that your Sun is in is how you express your core identity—the part of you that shines in the world and acts. Think of the Sun itself—fiery, sometimes

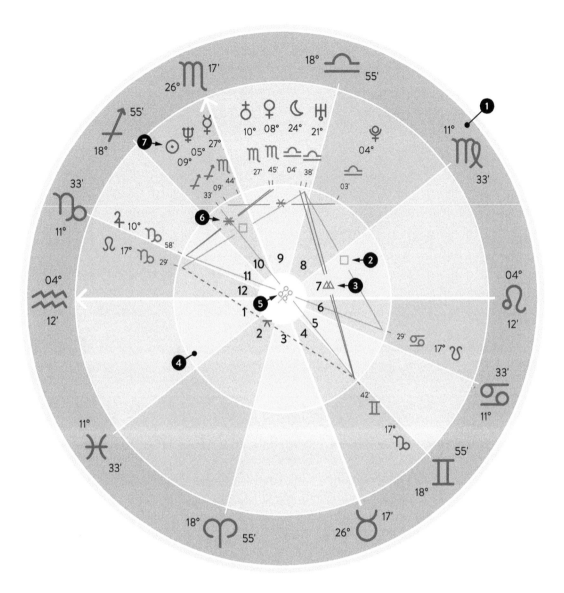

LEGEND: **1**. Signs; **2**. Square Aspect; **3**. Trine Aspect; **4**. Houses by number, counterclockwise; **5**. Opposition Aspect; **6**. Sextile Aspect; **7**. Planets

Sample Natal Chart. The chart is a wheel, or mandala, divided into 12 segments, or houses. Each house is ruled by a zodiac sign and represents a specific area of life. The chart shows the placement of planets and other celestial bodies within the zodiac based on the date, time, and location of a person's birth. The connecting lines in the middle are the aspects.

explosive, life-giving, and golden. How your Sun sign expresses itself is your light in the world. For example, in the sample chart, the Sun in Sagittarius will express itself most often as the freedom-seeking wanderer and wonderer but will also, at times, exhibit blind faith and moralistic tendencies. The aspects of the Sagittarius Sun sign you reflect is a free will choice.

While the Sun is obviously one of the most important parts of the chart, it should not be viewed in isolation. The Sun is your core identity, but it is not the totality of who you are. It is always tempered by the other placements in the chart.

In the sample chart, the Sagittarius Sun has an Aquarius Ascendant, meaning that this freedom seeker also comes across as being unique and as one who thinks differently. This person also has a Libra Moon, which gives an emotional attachment to harmony and peace. You would also look at the mix of elements in the chart. The Sun sign (which is a Fire sign), the Ascendant (which is an Air sign), and the Libra Moon would make this person a thinker and always on the move, as the air fans the flames of the fire. The Sagittarius Sun in the tenth house (see pages 26–28 for a deeper discussion of the houses) suggests this person enjoys being out in the world. A natural leader, they are also very career-oriented.

Awareness of these placements might make it easier for the person to understand their need for freedom and intellectual stimulation, and this would lead to acceptance that they are not suited to any work or experiences that are repetitive and without mental stimulation.

A deep understanding and acceptance of your Sun sign helps you understand how your ego shows up in the world. It is, however, through this understanding

Do You Know Your Sun Sign?

The dates for the Sun in each sign change yearly by a few days because they are based on the moment the Sun moves into a new sign. That moment can vary from the 18th to the 23rd of the month, so if you were born near the cusp (the starting point) of a sign, it is important to create a natal chart based on your own birth date. The dates given for each sign in part two are only a guide.

of the sign and house that your Sun is in that you begin to have a greater awareness of your choices. There might be times that it is appropriate to your needs to
embody one quality slightly more than the other. The constructs of positive and
negative are not always set in stone, so try not to consider those black-and-white
terms as you deepen your knowledge.

THE MOON ☾

In your chart, the Moon is your emotional body. It's a reflective and receptive
energy that responds and reacts. The Moon is your instinctive and intuitive self
and how you unconsciously respond to the world around you. Whereas the Sun
is your ego and the part of you that shines in the world and acts, the Moon is
your soul, your most private yet most connected, reactive self.

The Moon is very much a feminine energy that acts in all of us. She is the
Mother, your female ancestors, your home, and how you see all these things.
She represents where you are coming from, your upbringing, and how you
felt and feel about the world around you. Her silvery glow corresponds to the
reflective, mirrorlike energy that is within you, and the face known as the "man
in the moon" shows her very human side, the side that is the most immediately
felt energy in the cosmos.

As children we are emotional beings; it is only as we develop that society
teaches us that being "too emotional" or "too reactive" are undesirable qualities. Yet we *are* emotional beings at the core of our soul. What would it be like
to allow more of that? To allow ourselves to feel to the full extent of our being?
This, in part, is what this book aims to teach—how you can reach a point of
deep acceptance in the way you operate emotionally, spiritually, and physically
while learning to take the higher road in all aspects of your chart. A deep understanding and acceptance of the sign and house placement and aspects of your
Moon help you understand *how* you respond and react to external stimuli in
the world.

When you reach that point of deep acceptance and understanding, you are
able to choose which path you take with awareness. For example, the Moon
rules Cancer. Is your Moon in Cancer? If so, you would understand that this
placement makes you more emotionally sensitive than some other signs and
more receptive to other people's feelings. Moon in Cancer folk are also more
inclined to be deeply nurturing and family oriented. None of these traits are

good or bad; they just are. But once you accept that they just are, your awareness helps you deal with the deep sensitivity rather than perceiving it as "wrong." Viewing astrology in this way is all about making choices with awareness based on the embodiment of your own energies. In this specific example, you can choose whether to have a good cry under the bedcovers or whether to treat yourself to a nice healing massage if you are feeling emotionally hurt. Neither choice is wrong, but one might feel like the healthier response to you.

In the sample chart, the Moon is in Libra, which suggests this person likes a beautiful, harmonious, and airy home. This person is a diplomat; they can see two sides in every story and are able to compromise in almost every situation. This can, however, also lead to smoothing things over when it might be better off to discuss them, as Libra Moons dislike confrontational energy.

THE ASCENDANT ASC

The Ascendant, or rising sign, in your chart is the birthline—the eastern horizon at the moment and place of birth, represented by the left side of the horizontal line on the natal chart. It is the sign on the eastern horizon from your perspective at the moment you were born. The Ascendant is on the cusp (start of) the first house.

The Ascendant is also known as the mask, or persona. Think of it as your receptionist, the front desk agent who meets people for the first time one-on-one, and the aspect of your character that is presented to or perceived by others. It represents your appearance or the way you represent yourself to the world. I prefer the term "receptionist" because there is nothing false about the Ascendant, as the word *mask* implies. It's merely the part of the complex self that gets seen first. For example, the sample chart has the Sun in Sagittarius, which suggests this person is a freedom-loving philosopher at their core. Coupled with an Aquarian Ascendant, this person will appear to be more radical and unique than those with other Ascendant signs.

The Descendant

The Descendant is the point opposite the Ascendant, on the cusp of the seventh house, and represents what you attract and are attracted to. It also represents the disowned self or rejected parts of the self. I have not gone into the Descendant in depth as the themes are covered by the description of the cusp of the seventh house (see page 27). The Descendant is where we find our significant partners in life, but that isn't necessarily based on their Sun sign. For example, if you have Leo on the Descendant (as shown in the sample chart), you are attracted to strong Leo energy, which may come from the Sun, Moon, Ascendant, or a few planets in Leo.

PLUTO ♇

Pluto is highly important in Evolutionary Astrology. By the sign and house that it resides in, Pluto indicates the core evolutionary desires and intentions of our past (unfinished business from prior lifetimes), and Pluto's polarity point (the opposite point in the chart) reflects the evolutionary intentions for this lifetime. For example, those born with Pluto in the first house are born with an innate sense of the self, but their soul's intent is to learn how to be less overpowering in relationships and allow more balance from the people they are in relationships with.

In the sample chart, Pluto is in the eighth house in Libra. This person has had many lifetimes where they have either been powerless or overpowering in relationships. Their soul's evolutionary intent in this lifetime is to move toward developing their own sense of self-worth and independence so that they no longer repeat patterns of power and powerlessness.

MOON'S NODES

The Moon's Nodes are two virtual points where the Moon's monthly orbit cuts across the Sun's annual path around the earth, known as the elliptic. The Nodes go hand in hand with Pluto, the soul's desire, as the evolutionary path from the South Node to North Node is *how* your soul begins to reach its desire in this lifetime: the Pluto polarity point, or the opposite point, in the chart. A deep understanding of the Moon's Nodes can unlock the whole chart and give you the evolutionary direction to work on for your personal development.

THE SOUTH NODE ☋

The South Node encompasses the soul's habits; it is the oldest energy in you. It's soul energy that may have come down through a long lineage or many lifetimes. It's the deep past from which you have come. It contains instinctive habits and qualities that your soul has collected over eons. Because of its unconscious and instinctive nature, our soul's intention is to become conscious of these habits and innate abilities.

The South Node is sometimes presented as a negative because of its unconscious nature, but I prefer to understand it as more of a default or deeply ingrained setting. The soul's temptation is to stay attached to it, which limits choices and perspective. The aim, therefore, is to loosen the unconscious attachment through awareness of both its gifts and limitations and make conscious movement toward the pull of the North Node.

THE NORTH NODE ☊

The North Node is the soul's new evolutionary direction. This direction is uncomfortable because it is not something we were born with. The aim in all our efforts toward personal growth is to achieve awareness and, through our choices, to balance the unconscious habits and traits of the South Node through development of the traits and habits of the North Node in the opposite sign. This is a conscious choice, usually begun around midlife, but it is often felt earlier, inspiring a sense of balance and wholeness often unavailable from any source.

Someone with their South Node in Aries in the third house is likely to have the soul habit of being a loner and of being very assertive or even verbally harsh and often perceives themselves as unequivocally right. Through conscious awareness and choice, that person can develop the habit of being more aware of the other and working in collaboration with others to connect to higher perspectives.

In the sample chart, the South Node is in Cancer in the sixth house and the North Node is in Capricorn in the twelfth house. This suggests a person whose soul habit is to nurture and serve has moved to a degree of overgiving and servitude. Their soul's purpose is to release the habit of overgiving and create boundaries so that they are able to connect in a more healthy way with the collective.

ASPECTS

Aspects are angular relationships, or the lines that connect the placements in the chart. They tie the story of you together to create a complete and integrated whole. Chapter 15 includes details for how to identify and work with the aspects, so there's no need to fully understand this information yet. For now, here is some starting information that may appear a little esoteric until you know more:

Aspects are usually seen as harmonic or dynamic. Squares (90°) and oppositions (180°) are usually seen as more challenging, but they also give more impetus and dynamism. Conjunctions (0°), sextiles (60°), and trines (90°) are seen as more harmonious, but also give less impetus for growth, with the conjunction being the strongest blending and the sextile being slightly more dynamic than the trine.

Aspects describe how the points of the chart work together. In the sample chart, the person has a sextile aspect from Jupiter in Capricorn to a Venus and Mars conjunction in Scorpio. While there is a lot to unpack in this aspect, one reading of it suggests that this person is able to bond well with people of all genders and could, in fact, be a leader who brings people together.

TRANSITS

Transits are where the planets are *now* in relation to where they *were* at the time of our birth, so these do not appear on your natal chart. The transiting planets make aspects to the natal planets and other points in the natal chart. There's more on transits in chapter 15, showing you how to integrate the current movement of the planets into your analysis of your chart to see how those planetary movements are triggers for personal growth. In other words, transits show what part of the soul is being given the opportunity to grow and develop, and how that can happen in the present time or the date specified.

For example, if your Sun is at 21° Aries on your natal chart in the fifth house, and Pluto is currently at 21° Capricorn, Pluto would be said to be transiting square to your Sun. You would also look at which house transiting Pluto sits in to see what area of life this is affecting. Using the descriptions and keywords and phrases offered, you can blend them to create the transformation that is possible through the transit.

The outer planetary transits (Pluto, Uranus, Neptune, Saturn, and Jupiter) are usually looked at first, as they are slower-moving planets and provide lasting growth and development. The inner or faster-moving planets (Sun through Mars) are used to refine the interpretation, as their effect is more immediate.

ELEMENTS, GENDER TRAITS, AND POLARITIES

Let's pause for a moment and take a general look at the balance of elements, the gender traits, and the polarities (opposites) of the signs and houses. This is important to get an overall feel for yourself before looking at the individual placements. For example, are you predominantly fire (that is, active and out-going), or do you have many planets in "female" designated signs? Do you have planets all in one area of the chart (focused) or lots of oppositions (more balanced but also more challenges)? Knowing this offers deeper awareness of your blueprint.

THE ELEMENTS

There are four elements—Fire, Earth, Air, and Water—and the zodiac is divided up into these elements by sign and house according to their traits. The elements and their general traits are as follows:

Fire

The Fire signs are Aries, Leo, and Sagittarius, and they rule the first, fifth, and ninth houses, respectively. People with planets in these signs and houses are more action-oriented, spontaneous, and energetic. They are also prone to burnout.

Earth

The Earth signs are Taurus, Virgo, and Capricorn, and they rule the second, sixth, and tenth houses, respectively. People with planets in these signs and houses are grounded, practical, and concerned with earthly responsibilities.

Air

The Air signs are Gemini, Libra, and Aquarius, and they rule the third, seventh, and eleventh houses, respectively. Air signs are of the mind, intellectual, and thought based. These people are communicators, analyzers, and highly curious.

Water

The Water signs are Cancer, Scorpio, and Pisces, and they rule the fourth, eighth, and twelfth houses, respectively. Water signs are more feelings-based, intuitive, fluid, sensitive, and receptive. Traits of empathy and compassion are high in these signs.

MASCULINE AND FEMININE TRAITS

Signs are often defined as either masculine or feminine, though these definitions are crude and limiting, as we all have both masculine and feminine traits within us. However, the signs and traits traditionally considered to be masculine or feminine are as follows:

Masculine

Masculine signs are Aries, Gemini, Leo, Libra, Sagittarius, and Aquarius. They are extroverted and more physical in nature. These signs are primarily focused on mental and active pursuits and exploring the outer world.

Feminine

Feminine signs are Taurus, Cancer, Virgo, Scorpio, Capricorn, and Pisces. They are introverted and with more inner strength than physicality. These signs are more receptive and more inclined to inner, intuitive pursuits.

POLARITIES

In astrology, polarities are natural oppositions of signs and houses. Polarities are useful because the opposition point to any issue is often where the resolution is found. Hence the importance of the Pluto polarity point regarding your evolutionary intentions for this lifetime, because the polarity (or opposite) point is where your soul desires to evolve.

As you move through the book and do the exercises, it will be helpful to look at the opposite sign and/or house for all placements because that is where you can find traits that can help you resolve any difficulties you have. For example, if you have Sun in Aries, you may have a tendency to be quick-tempered and inconsiderate of others. By choosing to consciously develop some Libra qualities, such as fairness and consideration of the other, you may be able to lessen your own rashness. The six sign polarities are:

- Aries/Libra
- Taurus/Scorpio
- Gemini/Sagittarius
- Cancer/Capricorn
- Leo/Aquarius
- Virgo/Pisces

The house polarities are:

- First/Seventh
- Second/Eighth
- Third/Ninth
- Fourth/Tenth
- Fifth/Eleventh
- Sixth/Twelfth

In the following section, the house polarities are included with the descriptions of the sign polarities because there are enough similarities for you to be able to use this section for both.

Aries/Libra (First/Seventh)

This is about the balance between the self and the other. It's about assertion, compromise, and asking who the self is in relationship with the other. If, for example, you have a lot of planets in the seventh house or Libra, assertiveness might be a lesson for you to learn, or you may swing too far and be too assertive. Balance between the two is always the aim.

Taurus/Scorpio (Second/Eighth)

Traditionally, this represents the balance between possessions/your money and other people's money or money that comes from others. In addition, at a soul level, this polarity is also an extension of the Aries/Libra polarity in that it is the balance between your self-worth, values, and bonded relationships with others.

Gemini/Sagittarius (Third/Ninth)

This polarity is about the mind. Gemini and the third house are about making sense of things, what you think and talk about, and your learning style (often spoken of as the lower mind). Sagittarius and the ninth house represents higher thought, higher education, and philosophy, making sense of the bigger-picture things in life: faith and belief.

Cancer/Capricorn (Fourth/Tenth)

This is about balance between your inner, private life, your emotional security, your public self (Cancer/fourth house), and how you are seen in the world—your visibility (Capricorn/tenth house).

Leo/Aquarius (Fifth/Eleventh)

This polarity is about the balance between personal self-expression, joy, and creativity in Leo/fifth house and the more objective, group, or social consciousness in Aquarius/eleventh house.

Virgo/Pisces (Sixth/Twelfth)

Virgo/sixth house represents the relationship to service and mentorship, as in how you serve and mentor, as well as in your daily routines and work. The Pisces/twelfth house is your relationship with chaos, seclusion, and fluidity.

THE HOUSES

There are 12 segments, or houses, in the chart; each one is ruled by a sign, as noted in the previous section, and represents a specific area of life, as described in the following sections. The chart is a wheel of life beginning at birth with the Ascendant and moves counterclockwise through to metaphorical maturity and death.

Whereas the planets are the *what* in your chart, the signs are the *how*—or how those planets work in you. The houses are the *where*, showing where in your life the planets and signs have most influence. Through the blending of the meaning of planet, sign, house, and aspects, you will get a clearer picture of your gifts and possible blocks to manifesting those gifts. This awareness gives you the choices as to how you evolve and grow.

There are six personal houses (first through sixth) and six interpersonal houses (seventh through twelfth). The personal houses are those that influence your personal and inner life more keenly. The interpersonal houses influence your relationships and public life.

FIRST HOUSE. The first house influences your life force, self-awareness, personality, and appearance; how others see you initially (what you project); your early abilities; and your birth. For example, if you have Saturn in the first house, you are likely to be disciplined and able to create good personal boundaries.

SECOND HOUSE. The second house influences your inner resources, self-esteem and self-worth, your values, your relationship to the body and natural world, and your ability to earn money and how you spend it. For example, if you have Neptune in this house, you are likely to have "body intuition" and feel things through touch or body sensations. Neptune absorbs and feels subconscious energy and Taurus has to do with the body and the natural world. An example of this would be a massage therapist who senses irregularities or imbalances while touching someone's body.

THIRD HOUSE. The third house influences communication and perception. It's the voice, writing, what you think and talk about, your learning style and early education, and your relationships with neighbors and siblings. For example, Mars in the third house would indicate a direct and clear communicator who can, at times, use words as a weapon.

FOURTH HOUSE. The fourth house influences the nature of your inner life, your basis of security, the home, family of origin, heredity or ancestry, and your relationship with one of your parents. For example, Jupiter in the fourth house could indicate an expansive inner life and/or a few home moves in your life.

FIFTH HOUSE. The fifth house influences self-expression, joy in living, love affairs, creativity, children, fun, romance, play, leisure, and pleasure. For example, Venus in this house is charming, energetic, and fun to be around, though there can be a tendency to think the world revolves around them and expect others to treat them as such.

SIXTH HOUSE. The sixth house influences service to others, mentoring, day-to-day work experience, health, daily routines, skills you learn, diet, and pets. For example, the Moon in the sixth house would indicate that the person has emotional needs for routine and to serve others.

SEVENTH HOUSE. The seventh house influences personal relationships; how people react to you; your relationship to significant others, including your partner; cooperation and collaboration; and your disowned self that you see in others. For example, Pluto in the seventh house can bring tendencies to be powerful in relationships or to attract those who overpower.

EIGHTH HOUSE. The eighth house influences intimacy (emotionally, psychologically, and sexually bonded relationships), the deep psyche, shamanism (a spiritual practice of altered consciousness), taboo subjects, death (physical and psychological), underlying reality and soul material, and shared resources. For example, those with the Sun in the eighth house are deeply passionate and their feelings run deep.

NINTH HOUSE. The ninth house influences the higher self, religion, philosophical beliefs, sources of expansion and illumination, higher learning, wisdom, long journeys, other cultures, and experience of the divine. For example, Mercury in the ninth house indicates one who loves to explore philosophy and cultures through higher study.

TENTH HOUSE. The tenth house influences your public self and reputation, your mission in this lifetime, how you are seen in the world, the nature of your career, visibility, power and status, and your relationship with one of your parents. For example, Mercury in the tenth house indicates an authoritative communicator who can, at times, tend to be bossy; this person is happiest in a career that involves communication.

ELEVENTH HOUSE. The eleventh house influences community, groups of friends, creative group expression, causes, social consciousness/politics, humanitarian endeavors, inventions and new ideas, the future, and the internet. For example, Uranus in the eleventh house indicates that this person is innovative and thrives on standing out from the crowd, but they can sometimes alienate others by doing so.

TWELFTH HOUSE. The twelfth house influences emotional responses and blocks; unconscious or altered states (dreams, trance meditation), mystery, magic, creativity, mysticism, seclusion, confinement, limitations, and restrictions. For example, someone with Mars in the twelfth house usually has a strong spiritual drive but often keeps their desires private.

ZODIAC QUALITIES

In astrology, we have three modalities, or modes of expression, with four signs in each modality. The modalities are cardinal, fixed, and mutable. For example, in the sample chart, the South Node, Pluto, Uranus, the Moon, Jupiter, and the North Node are in cardinal signs; Venus, Mars, and Mercury are in fixed signs; and Saturn, Neptune, and the Sun are in mutable signs. We generally give slightly more weight to the Sun and the Moon (one point for each placement, and three points each for the Sun and the Moon), so this person is primarily cardinal, which means they are a great initiator.

Look at your chart to see which modalities your planets are in and which houses you have them in to see which modality is your strongest and which is your weakest.

CARDINAL

Cardinal signs are initiators; they like new beginnings and new projects. The cardinal signs are Aries, Cancer, Libra, and Capricorn, and the cardinal houses are the first, fourth, seventh, and tenth (the beginning of each quadrant of the chart).

FIXED

Fixed signs are stable and enduring; they fix things in place and are good finishers. The fixed signs are Taurus, Leo, Scorpio, and Aquarius, and the fixed houses are the second, fifth, eighth, and eleventh (the middle of each quadrant of the chart).

MUTABLE

Mutable signs are adaptable and flexible but can also be the shape-shifters of the zodiac, changing to fit the outer circumstances. The mutable signs are Gemini, Virgo, Sagittarius, and Pisces, and the mutable houses are the third, sixth, ninth, and twelfth (the end of each quadrant of the chart).

DIGGING INTO THE ZODIAC

There are neither good nor bad qualities in the Self. The Self is free from all qualities. Qualities pertain to the mind only. —SRI RAMANA MAHARSHI

In part two, we'll be looking at each sign through the lens of growth and how to integrate that energy with some of the other elements in the chart. While it is tempting to apply these chapters to your Sun sign, I encourage you to get to know all the energies in the chart and apply them to wherever they show up in your chart, because we each have every sign in our chart, even if there is greater or lesser emphasis because of planetary placements.

In the sample chart, Aries is on the cusp the third house. So, for this chart, we would want to blend the meaning of the Aries traits and the third house qualities even though there are no planets in that house. I would say that this person is a direct and assertive communicator and a very clear thinker who might be resistant to listening to other people's points of view. There are other ways to word this, but this gives you a feel for how we begin to blend the sign and house. (After you have read this book and have done the exercises for each sign, turn to Appendix A on page 213 to read a case study where I show you an example of how to blend everything you've learned.)

In astrological terms, traits are often described as positive and negative, shine and shadow, or higher and lower. These are value judgments, however, and the aim of this book is to see them as elements of the self that can be perceived either way. In other words, a so-called negative trait can sometimes be a useful, positive trait. Using astrology in this way brings awareness and choice in regard to how you embody and develop the energies in your chart. Remember, this is not about anything being broken; it is about making choices with awareness based on the embodiment of your own energies. There are always choices. Throughout this book, I show how you can make different choices within each area of your chart. As I mentioned earlier, neither choice is better or worse; it is just a choice. With the knowledge you get from your natal chart, you can choose with awareness.

We begin navigating the cosmic energies through the lens of the signs because we have to begin somewhere and, as previously mentioned, the Sun sign is the most easily identifiable. The goal, however, is for you to use the trait descriptions and words to create a blended picture that reveals where you can use your awareness and free will to choose which direction you wish to develop in based on your cosmic blueprint. This means that you will be working in alignment with your soul's blueprint in this lifetime, which takes away much of the need for outer guidance. In other words, your awareness will enable you to make your own personal choices based on your individual soul self.

As we go through each sign in the following chapters, I approach the discussions by speaking to the symbology and its shamanic meanings. I also bring in some mythology. You will take a shamanic journey (a form of active meditation in which you explore your mind rather than trying to empty it) to each planet using your imagination to help you understand and embody its energy more deeply. You will also have opportunities to journal your insights and reflections. (I suggest you get a journal designated for the exercises in this book.) Looking at and exploring the energies this way offers a deep understanding of the energy—more than you can get from the abstract process of reviewing a mere list of words.

PART TWO

the zodiac

aries
the ram

The most powerful weapon on earth is the human soul on fire. —FERDINAND FOCH

Dates: March 20–April 20, depending on the year

ELEMENT	MODALITY	RULING PLANET	HOUSE RULED
Fire	Cardinal	Mars	First

Aries is a cardinal Fire sign and is ruled by Mars. It's the first sign of the zodiac, which is a great indicator of the nature of Aries.

Aries is represented by the Ram. Rams have long been seen as a symbol of determination. The Aries glyph represents the Ram's horns, and in shamanic practices, the horns are thought to stimulate mental activity. Rams are powerful, strong, and well-known for butting heads in duels of strength. Their magnificent horns are status symbols as well as weapons. This is all reflected in Aries energy.

Aries energy is independent, spontaneous, enthusiastic, entrepreneurial, aggressive, impulsive, and energizing. They are hardheaded leaders who aren't afraid to take the initiative. Aries energy has a healthy self-interest, which can, at times, verge on being all about "me." Sometimes it is a good thing to be self-centered, and sometimes less so. People with Aries energy need to learn to courageously put themselves first as they may have experienced past-life situations where they felt trapped or were prevented from doing so.

As a cardinal sign, Aries is doubly initiating, self-starting, raw, honest, and motivated by a challenge. Both Aries energy and cardinal energy are pioneering; they like to blaze new trails. This is energy that stirs things up—for example, the motivational speaker who inspires others into action. They often go toward their fears, usually in an attempt to conquer innate fears from the past. They are, however, poor finishers due to impatience, so they work best when they can start things and delegate or be accountable to someone else.

Aries likes a challenge and often takes risks; otherwise, they feel impatient and volatile. Aries knows what they like and want and doesn't like to waste time on anything or anyone that isn't a fit for them. The healthy way to use this energy is to take the lead and initiate projects. For example, the Sun in Aries in the eleventh house might mean that the person is driven to lead communities and groups, or the Sun in Aries in the ninth house might make the person a religious leader or someone who is certain of their truth.

In an unaware state (someone who has little self-awareness and usually looks outside of themselves for answers), Aries energy can be reactive and nitpicking, with a great need to always be first or right. With awareness and choice, Aries energy turns toward healthy self-interest and lives a life of self-challenge rather than challenging others. It's good to be self-centered when an Aries is constantly daring themselves to take on something that scares and challenges them. They are fulfilling their potential, thereby inspiring others.

Now that you have a general feel for Aries energy, we'll look at *how* the planets show up in Aries and the houses. With your chart in hand, look for *which* planets you have in Aries, *how* the planets work in that sign, and *where* in the chart they are—the house. Then you will blend the energies by identifying keywords and phrases from all three that have meaning for you, remembering that you can replace them with any synonyms or phrases with the same meaning of your choosing. With this list, you will create a coherent and meaningful picture to get a deep understanding of how Aries energy manifests within you. This is where the real awareness and choice comes in. Armed with this knowledge, you can choose how you respond and react to Aries energy and how you manifest it in the world.

PLANETS IN ARIES

This section gives you a brief description of each planet in the sign Aries. I encourage you not to treat these discussions as definitive descriptions, but as a springboard for your own interpretation using similar words and themes. You are invited to use these descriptions and the exercises in this chapter to create your own description of how the energy of Aries and the planets show up within you.

MOON IN ARIES

The Moon represents your emotional body, and in Aries, the emotions can be as fiery as they come. Prone to sudden outbursts that are over as fast as they began, this placement could be seen as the toddler of the zodiac—in the best way possible. Emotionally impulsive and pleasure seeking, Aries Moons like their needs met in the moment. There's zero passive aggression with Moon in Aries, and this person will express their emotions clearly, but sometimes that can cut like a knife. If you have Moon in Aries, know that you can choose to pause before reacting so that you have a moment to consider your response to emotional triggers.

MERCURY IN ARIES

Mercury represents communications, and in Aries, words are clear, concise, and direct. Ideas are expressed passionately and often without pausing for thought. Always open to and creating new concepts, Mercury in Aries is a pioneering thought leader. Sometimes, their directness can be hard to take by others because cooperation and listening are not their strongest points. They are, however, courageous, innovative, and inspiring at their strongest. If you have Mercury in Aries, listening to other people's points of view will help you learn to see other perspectives.

VENUS IN ARIES

Venus represents love, relationships, pleasure, creativity, and the value we place on the material things in life and our own pleasure. Venus in Aries is bold, fun, and goes after what they want. They love freshness and excitement in all relationships and in the material world. This can be a little too much for some, but if you have Venus in Aries, your soul's desire in this lifetime is to create relationships that help you develop your courageous and loving nature. You wish to learn how to be deeply accepting of your need to have this excitement while also coming from a place of accepting other people's needs (without diminishing your raw energy).

MARS IN ARIES

Mars is the ruling planet of Aries, and therefore its energy is in alignment with Aries energy. Mars represents your will, your drive, and your vigor. In Aries, these qualities are amped up, resulting in being highly strong-willed, driven, energetic, and competitive. When repressed, this can lead to anger and aggression; learn instead to apply this energy with courage and directness. Direct it toward what you desire rather than push against what you don't desire.

JUPITER IN ARIES

Jupiter represents expansion, faith, truth, and freedom, but also grandiosity. Jupiter in Aries is about faith in yourself and your truth and actions. Taken to its limit, this is about believing that only your truth is valid and thinking you have all the answers to life's philosophical questions. If you have Jupiter in Aries, growth will come from continuing the quest for truth through exposure to the unfamiliar, exposure to other people's truth and faith in themselves, and standing up for what you believe while recognizing that others have the right to their own beliefs.

SATURN IN ARIES

Saturn represents mastery, determination, and discipline. Both Saturn and Aries represent leadership, so this combination makes for very strong leadership abilities. Saturn in Aries is able to overcome seemingly impossible odds to achieve their desires and loves trying and mastering new things. Saturn gives Aries staying power. This is a powerful combination. By keeping in mind that benevolent leadership gets the best results, you will inspire others rather than try to overpower them.

URANUS IN ARIES

Uranus represents individuality, unpredictability, and unconventionality. Uranus in Aries can be genius energy, innovative and inspiring but constantly changing, rebellious, and erratic. Because Uranus also represents the higher mind, if you have Uranus in Aries, you may be prone to mental stress and anxiety. Grounding meditations or time in nature can help soothe some of the irascibility.

NEPTUNE IN ARIES

Neptune represents inspiration, illusion, psychic sensitivity, healing, and confusion. Neptune in Aries is a creative and, at times, radical visionary who initiates big dreams. They can get so focused on this dream that they lose some details along the way. If you have Neptune in Aries, you may find that you work best with someone who can help you pick up the details, but not control the overall vision, as you are very focused on the vision.

PLUTO IN ARIES

Pluto is the soul or the soul's desire. Pluto spends approximately 20 years in each sign, so the mighty dwarf planet's influence is generational, meaning that everyone in a generation will have Pluto in the same sign. The house placement must be blended with the generational concepts to get a clear picture for your own cosmic blueprint.

Pluto was in Aries from 1822 to 1853 and returns in 2068; therefore, no one alive has Pluto in Aries. However, those with Pluto in Aries are likely to be those who are prepared to go to extremes to get what they desire. Pluto's themes of power and transformation are likely to display themselves more directly with these individuals than any other sign due to the directness of Aries energy. It is a powerful combination. Mark Twain, Claude Monet, and Thomas Edison were all born with Pluto in Aries.

SOUTH NODE IN ARIES

If you have the South Node in Aries, you are learning to release the instinctive soul habit of having a "me first" mentality, aggression, too much self-reliance, selfishness, and acting without considering the consequences. As the South Node habits are so instinctual, they often display the more unconscious or unaware traits of the sign.

NORTH NODE IN ARIES

If you have the North Node in Aries, you are looking to become more self-reliant, developing your leadership abilities, prioritizing your own wishes, and learning to express anger in an open and healthy manner, leaving behind passive-aggressive behavior or codependence.

Shamanic Journey to Mars, Ruler of Aries

In this exercise, you are going to journey to non-ordinary reality, the upper world, in a practice called shamanic journey work. This is similar to a meditation but enables you to actively ask for guidance and answers. Shamanic journey work is an amazing practice for getting support in life. You can take a shamanic journey as often as you would like.

For this journey, search the term "Shamanic Drumming" on YouTube or your preferred video-streaming platform. Pick a track that is 10 to 15 minutes long. (I especially enjoy tracks by Shamanic Experience or Sandra Ingerman.) Experiment with two or three and decide which one feels right for you. It is best to listen using headphones or on high volume. Start the track once you have gotten comfortable.

Either lie on a comfortable blanket or sit comfortably with both feet on the ground. Start the track, and close your eyes.

Picture yourself in a starting place. Mine is a meadow, but yours might be a beach, a mountain, a forest, or any other place. Always trust what comes to you.

When you have pictured yourself in that place, look around to see if you have any spirit guides with you (commonly animals or other allies, which might include mythical creatures or even plants and trees). Ask your spirit guide to journey with you. Next, look for a way to the upper world. It might be a ladder, stairs, or a beanstalk, or you may simply fly. Again, trust what comes to you.

Now, imagine yourself journeying to Mars, the ruler of Aries. Take note of everything that happens. Have a conversation with Mars by asking questions.

How can Mars help you grow in the area of your chart where Mars and/or Aries are?

How can Mars and Aries support you with your personal growth?

Mars might respond by suggesting how you can be less reactive in areas of your chart or, alternatively, how you can develop the energies of Mars and Aries to help you embody them in your chart. Remember, this is a conversation where you are seeking to develop your energies in the best way possible for you.

When the conversation is over, thank Mars and return to your starting place. When you are ready to open your eyes, journal about your experience.

ARIES THROUGH THE HOUSES

The house where Aries falls in your natal chart brings deeper insights into those areas of life where you take initiative and action. This is where you naturally lead and take aligned action but also where you may express anger. Bring your awareness to how you might be controlling and/or unaware of other people's views and actions in this area of life.

ARIES IN THE FIRST HOUSE

If you have Aries in or on the cusp of the first house, you are a human *doing*, always on the go, very physical, and highly self-oriented. You always have to be first, and you are or will be a great leader. The evolutionary challenge of this placement is to learn collaboration and cooperation with others, which doesn't come naturally here (unless other chart placements show that it does), and to lead by example.

ARIES IN THE SECOND HOUSE

Aries in or on the cusp of the second house gives you the ability to embody high self-worth and self-esteem. Sometimes this is through the lens of generating wealth and material items that prove your worth to the world. The evolutionary, or growth, impulse here is to realize that true self-worth comes from within by embodying leadership and inner strength of character.

ARIES IN THE THIRD HOUSE

If you have Aries in or on the cusp of the third house, you are a clear and concise communicator and a fast learner. You make an excellent teacher if you can resist the temptation to be impatient, as well as the urge to do things for others rather than let them take in information and act at their own pace.

ARIES IN THE FOURTH HOUSE

If you have Aries in or on the cusp of the fourth house, you will likely have created an identity separate from the home at a young age. You will separate from family conditioning at an earlier age than any other sign in the fourth house. You are very much your own person. You are at your happiest taking control and doing things around the home, and the temptation will be to push others to do the same or to do everything for them rather than allowing them to develop at their own pace. As the fourth house also represents your inner self, you are likely to be very self-demanding. Allow others to do things to lighten the load and in their own way. Keep in mind the image of a benevolent leader in the home.

ARIES IN THE FIFTH HOUSE

Aries in or on the cusp of the fifth house enjoys physical activity and active play and creativity. You are likely to be the leader at the party and in love affairs, lots of fun, and full of life force. If you have children, you are likely to be somewhat demanding, which may not be a good fit for all children, or your own children will be strong-willed. Overall, this is a Fire sign in a fiery house, so everything is infused with passion.

ARIES IN THE SIXTH HOUSE

If you have Aries in or on the cusp of the sixth house, you are likely to be driven in your daily and work routines—the kind of person who is highly organized and on the go at all times. As this is also the house of service and mentorship, you will make an excellent leader in these areas. It's important, however, not to make your service all about you; make it about the service instead. It's also important to learn to delegate successfully as you are susceptible to burnout and health problems if you try to do everything yourself.

ARIES IN THE SEVENTH HOUSE

Aries in or on the cusp of the seventh house indicates that you are very direct in your significant relationships. You are attracted to those who are independent and active, or you will seek to control and take over others in your significant relationships. Your relationships are likely to be passionate and fiery, which can also lead to the Ram-like locking of horns at times. The image of people standing side by side and supporting each other fully, neither dominating the other, is a good one to hold.

ARIES IN THE EIGHTH HOUSE

If you have Aries in or on the cusp of the eighth house, you have the potential to benefit from the actions of those you are in closely bonded relationships with. Abundance may come through other people's actions, and that can affect the Aries sense of self, as Aries likes to do everything themselves. On the other hand, you may become a leader in the metaphysical world, fearlessly delving into the deepest of places and leading others into those magical places.

ARIES IN THE NINTH HOUSE

If you have Aries in or on the cusp of the ninth house, you are a leader in concepts of the higher mind, philosophy, truth, and freedom. Aries is such an enthusiastic energy, however, there is a tendency to get dogmatic around those beliefs and to teach that yours is the only way or truth. Ideally this energy would be turned to the higher self and helping others explore their own higher self through teaching different philosophies.

ARIES IN THE TENTH HOUSE

If you have Aries in or on the cusp of the tenth house, your self-concept is tied up with your career and/or mission in life. You are likely to be driven by public and professional recognition, and others will be measuring you by your public actions and roles. With both the tenth house and Aries being about the "I am" concept (both one-on-one and publicly with regard to leadership), you may be an autocratic leader unless you temper your actions to consider others.

ARIES IN THE ELEVENTH HOUSE

If you have Aries in or on the cusp of the eleventh house, you are inspired to action by groups and humanitarian causes or to lead others. You are very sociable and have large groups of friends and love spending time with them, usually leading activities and groups. These bonds are unlikely to be lasting, as Aries has trouble finding groups that can keep up with the constant seeking of new experiences—or there may be clashes with others who also want to take the lead. Heart-opening meditations can help slow you down and deepen your connection with others.

As Aries is all about self-concept and identity, you can get a little lost in or on the cusp of the twelfth house, which represents the collective unconscious and connection to the muse and mystery. Here, Aries energy can be squelched or dampened by others. There may be an inability to take action for yourself or on behalf of others. Growth will come from the realization that the "I" is, in fact, connected to all that is, and therefore, that identification with the collective helps you see yourself in that collective, allowing you to serve selflessly without losing your sense of self.

Aries Strategies to Improve Communication Skills

Aries think and act quickly and are very self-focused, creating a tendency to shut down open paths of communication because they don't take the time to think of or listen to others. The following strategies will help you improve your communication skills.

1. Consciously give your undivided attention to the people you communicate with. Make an effort to stay present and keep your mind from wandering to other things. This will greatly improve how your words are received.

2. Pause after you speak to give others the opportunity to respond, and take time to listen to them and really hear what they are saying.

3. Be mindful of *how* you are communicating. Your body language and your tone can make a big difference in how people perceive you, and Aries can unwittingly appear quite intimidating. Soften your posture and tone if you wish your words to be well received. Slowing down the rate at which you speak is also helpful.

ARIES CASE STUDY

Sarah has the following placements in her chart:

- Sun in Aries in the seventh house
- Moon in Libra in the second house
- Virgo Ascendant

In this example, we are looking only at the Sun, Moon, and Ascendant, but the case study in Appendix A on page 213 integrates other elements in the natal chart.

Sarah needs to make an important decision and is having problems with indecisiveness. This is not uncommon for someone with a Libra Moon. Through her work with her natal chart, Sarah has identified herself as a pioneer (Sun in the seventh house) who is emotionally inclined to be a peacemaker (Libra Moon emphasized by the Sun in the seventh house) and has the persona of someone who is a trustworthy perfectionist (Virgo Ascendant). With a Libra Moon in the second house and the Sun in the seventh house, Sarah's independent Aries Sun is tempered by collaborative placements and the service energy of the Ascendant.

To assist her in making this important decision, her chart suggests that she gently move her focus to single-mindedness (Aries) to examine how she is helping others (Virgo service).

THE SOUL IN ARIES

The personality and behavior of Aries, or any Sun sign, is affected by all the other placements and aspects in the natal chart. This is why it is important to gradually blend the meanings of the planets, signs, houses, aspects, and transits to create an overall picture of the potential in your personal blueprint.

If Aries is your Sun sign, you may have things in common with other Aries Sun signs, but you are uniquely you. For example, an Aries Sun with Cancer Ascendant will be a lot more private and even appear shy compared with an Aries Sun with Capricorn Ascendant who would appear quite stern and reserved. Another example is a person with an Aries Sun and Aries Moon, who would be fiery and more assertive than a person with an Aries Sun and Scorpio Moon, who would be more likely to internalize emotions. This is why it is so key to gradually blend the planets, signs, houses, aspects, and transits to create an overall picture of the potential in your blueprint.

Mars and Aries Journaling Exercise

Choose a quiet time and place to look at your natal chart and have your journal handy. Identify Mars and Aries in your chart. Look at the sign placement of Mars and the house placement of both Mars and Aries. You can look at Aries in the houses (see page 39) to get a feel for what Mars in the houses may also mean.

In your journal, write down keywords and phrases from this book and from your shamanic journey to Mars. Reflect on how you manifest these energies in your life and how you might choose to develop these energies in a more conscious rather than reactive way. For example, you may have Mars or Aries in the fifth house and find yourself being overly controlling with your children, if you have any, or losing your temper quickly. Through this awareness, you might choose to create a pause (a simple inner count to three or a deep breath) before reacting to triggers that cause your temper to flare. Record your reflections in your journal.

Through this journaling exercise and your shamanic journey to Mars, you will begin to really understand the energies in your chart. Through that awareness, you will be able to choose *how* you embody the energies of Mars and Aries in your life.

Here are a few things to consider to help you to make the most of your Aries energy in different areas of life. Always consider that your soul chose the Aries energy so that you could be more energetic, passionate, and assertive in that area of life. You can choose to maximize the positive energies of Aries.

GENERAL PERSONAL DEVELOPMENT

The issue that causes the most problems for Aries is their reactivity and tendency to lose their temper. Of course, sometimes this is a good thing as Aries is learning to express themselves without suppressing their natural instincts. However, learning to pause before reacting can help mature this aspect of the self so that you are responding rather than reacting without consciousness.

RELATIONSHIPS/RELATING TO OTHERS

In any analysis of your chart placements, it is helpful to look at the opposite sign for answers, and this is especially true when looking at relationships. For Aries, that opposite sign is Libra, the sign of collaboration, cooperation, and listening/mediation. This isn't to suggest that you should become completely like Libra—only that you should infuse some of these qualities in your dealings with others to have more successful relationships.

ACHIEVING GOALS

Aries is excellent at setting goals and going after what they want. It's actually sustaining the effort to achieve the goals that is more difficult for them. To help you with this, look to where Saturn is in your chart and work with those energies or find those who can hold your "feet to the fire" (i.e., hold you accountable) to keep working on that goal.

CAREERS

For a full analysis of what type of career you would be suited to, take into account the cusp of the tenth house (the Midheaven), the ruler of that sign, and any planets in the tenth house. For example, someone with an Aries Sun in the third house with Scorpio on the cusp of the tenth house and Pluto, ruler of Scorpio, conjunct the Ascendant in Capricorn would be suited to a career like therapy, surgery, or science (Scorpio in the tenth house) and things that explore the unknown. They also have the potential to be a powerful authority in these subjects (Pluto/Capricorn Ascendant).

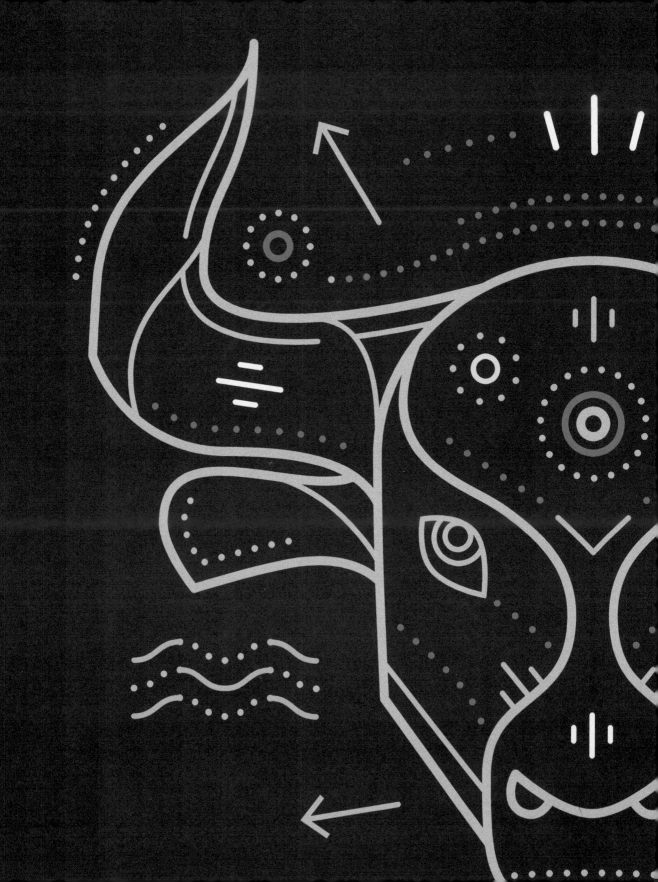

taurus the bull

All our wisdom is stored in the trees. —SANTOSH KALWAR

Dates: April 20–May 20, depending on the year

ELEMENT	MODALITY	RULING PLANET	HOUSE RULED
Earth	Fixed	Venus	Second

Taurus is a fixed Earth sign and is ruled by Venus. It's the second sign in the zodiac, and it is where we begin to embody the "I am" energy and become aware of our physicality and connection to the physical world.

Taurus is represented by the Bull, which has long been a symbol for fertility. In many cultures, the Bull became a symbol of fertility through sacrifice. Bulls have also appeared in many mythological legends. The Egyptian god Osiris is often depicted with the head of a bull, and one of the best-known Greek legends is that of the Minotaur, part man and part bull.

The Bull symbolizes strength of purpose and solidity. Bulls are abundant and fertile; they are also slow and steady unless angered. Usually tenacious, hardworking, and patient, the notion of the "raging bull" shows how Taurus may respond when angered. The glyph for Taurus is believed to represent the Sun (the male) with the horns as crescent moons (the female), indicating fertility and fecundity.

Like the Bull, Taurus energy embodies animal wisdom. Taurus people are natural builders, patient, practical, and loyal and have an innate relationship to the body and material world. Whereas Aries starts things, Taurus brings about tangible form and preserves. As a fixed sign, Taurus is sustaining, reliable, and determined, willing to do whatever it takes to create what they set out to do. There's a solid quality to Taurus energy that can be immovable at times—the more you push, the more Taurus resists. Taurus is the most present of signs, happy to sit in silence and allowing the self to feel the earth, the surroundings, and just *be*.

Taurus has a sensual quality. Many people with a Taurus Sun sign gain understanding through touch and enjoy good food, comfortable surroundings, ambient temperatures, and material comforts. They also tend to be independent emotionally and financially, and find it difficult to understand those who aren't. For example, if someone has their Sun in Taurus in the third house, it might mean they are deliberate in their thought processing, but also often resistant to changing their mind. Or possessing the Sun in Taurus in the fifth house would make someone a consistent and affectionate parent, but they may have a tendency to be rigid in their expectations.

In an unaware state, Taurus energy can be possessive, stubborn, and stuck through a need for physical security. Their often wonderful quality of letting nothing get in their way can become a less positive one when it involves accumulation for the sake of accumulation. Taurus can be self-indulgent to the degree that they just aren't aware of other people's emotions. With awareness, Taurus can choose to relax their hold on things, ideas, and people.

Now let's look at *how* the planets show up in Taurus and the houses. With your chart in hand, look for *which* planets you have in Taurus, *how* the planets work in that sign, and *where* in the chart they are—the house. Then you will blend the energies by identifying keywords and phrases from all three that have meaning for you, remembering that you can replace them with any synonyms or phrases with the same meaning of your choosing. With this list, you will create a coherent and meaningful picture to get a deep understanding of how Taurus energy manifests within you. This is where the real awareness and choice comes in. Armed with this knowledge, you can choose how you respond and react to Taurus energy and how you manifest it in the world.

PLANETS IN TAURUS

This section gives you a brief description of each planet in the sign Taurus. I encourage you not to treat these discussions as definitive descriptions but as a springboard for your own interpretation using similar words and themes. You are invited to use these descriptions and the exercises in this chapter to create your own description of how the energy of Taurus and the planets show up within you.

MOON IN TAURUS

The Moon represents your emotional body. In Taurus, the emotions are mellow. Both Taurus and the Moon are receptive energies; therefore, Taurus Moons are responsive rather than active and are resistant to change. Those with a Taurus Moon love security and solidity in their lives and those they surround themselves with. The main pleasure-seekers of the zodiac, they are usually a joy to be around because they make relaxation a priority. If you have a Taurus Moon, be aware of when you are fixated on something and resistant to change because you feel pushed. Check into your inner self and ask if this change would actually be the right thing for you.

MERCURY IN TAURUS

Mercury represents communication and thought processes, and in Taurus, both of these processes are slow and deliberate. They take in information through the senses as they listen, observe, touch (if appropriate), taste, and feel. They trust tangible ideas and information that aligns with natural law, which can be a challenge in a world so out of alignment with nature's cycles. Mercury in Taurus usually has a melodious voice that others love to listen to and often make great singers and presenters. If you have Mercury in Taurus, others may see your deliberation as frustrating and even lazy, so it is helpful to actually express that you need time to solidify your thoughts and ideas.

VENUS IN TAURUS

Venus represents love, relationships, pleasure, creativity, and the value we place on the material things in life and our pleasure. Venus, in its earthly, material form, is the ruling planet of Taurus, and, as such, the energies of each are in alignment. These people are strong, sensual, dislike drama, and can be slow to commit, but once they do, they are loyal and even possessive. This applies to relationships as well as other physical possessions. Venus in Taurus can appear reserved while they take their time processing whether a person or thing comes with drama. They are attracted to pleasing physical appearances but will always take time to look beyond that, as they also want quality in everything they own. The only real downside of this placement is that they will hold on to things and people, even when the time for that possession has passed. Developing the ability to know when it is time to let go is a useful practice if you have Venus in Taurus.

MARS IN TAURUS

Mars represents your will, your drive, and your energy. In Taurus, these energies have great staying power and determination, and a person with Mars in Taurus will work steadily toward their goals with focus, no matter how long it takes. They will also not take on more than they can manage. The immovable energy of Taurus is especially strong here as both Mars and Taurus are so focused. This can make this placement resistant to change even if the goal they are working toward isn't coming into being. Learning that it is sometimes useful to make adjustments and shift tracks is a helpful skill to adopt if you have this placement.

JUPITER IN TAURUS

Jupiter represents expansion, faith, truth, and freedom but also grandiosity. Jupiter is abundant and strong in creative Taurus. These people are able to create abundance and material wealth with relative ease, and they revel in the finer things of life and can have a tendency to overindulge in all things that bring them pleasure. They will also be attracted to ideologies that bring practical results and make changes in the material world. When you are aware of the power of Jupiter in Taurus, you are able to choose generosity over accumulation and share your abundant nature with others.

SATURN IN TAURUS

Saturn represents mastery, determination, and discipline. Both Saturn and Taurus are earthly and exhibit determination and staying power, yet little comes easy with this placement; they have to work hard for everything they get, and, as the shadow of Saturn is fear of not being enough, they have a tendency to drive themselves harder than any other placement and even deny themselves the fruits of their labors. If you have this placement, a reevaluation of and focus on your individual core values can help relax the "hard" quality of Saturn in Taurus and enhance your enjoyment of your achievements along the way.

URANUS IN TAURUS

Uranus represents individuality, unpredictability, and unconventionality. With Uranus in Taurus, the steady energy gets a boost of get-up-and-go with an ability to come up with innovative ideas and methods. This placement can seem to be more open to change than other Taurus placements, but we must remember that Uranus rules Aquarius, another fixed sign, so their inventive quality can lead to a stubborn streak once they have decided their course of action. With this placement, learning to be more flexible and open to other people's ideas would be helpful to you.

NEPTUNE IN TAURUS

Neptune represents inspiration, illusion, psychic sensitivity, healing, and confusion. Neptune in Taurus has visionary ideals connected to money and material resources and is often able to make their vision real. They have an almost psychic connection to nature and possessions and often have intuition that involves physical connection to the world—that is, by touch. However, the nebulous and illusory nature of Neptune can lead to depression if you find yourself unable to bring your ideas to fruition, so keep an eye out for symptoms and seek help as necessary.

PLUTO IN TAURUS

Pluto is the soul or the soul's desire. Pluto spends approximately 20 years in each sign, so the mighty dwarf planet's influence is generational, which means that everyone in a generation is influenced by the sign that Pluto is in. The house placement must be blended with the generational concepts to get a clear picture for your own natal cosmic blueprint.

Pluto was in Taurus from 1853 to 1885 and returns in 2098. There is no one currently alive who was born during this time. Those born with Pluto in Taurus brought wealth transformation in a powerfully persistent and logical way. Pluto in Taurus relentlessly goes after what it wants but often ignores underlying forces in its determination to create. Carl Jung, Sigmund Freud, Mahatma Gandhi, and Albert Einstein were all born with Pluto in Taurus.

Shamanic Journey to Venus, Ruler of Taurus

In this exercise you are going to journey to non-ordinary reality, the upper world, in a practice called shamanic journey work. This is similar to a meditation but enables you to actively ask for guidance and answers. Shamanic journey work is an amazing practice for getting support in life. You can take a shamanic journey as often as you would like.

For this journey, search the term "Shamanic Drumming" on YouTube or your preferred video-streaming platform. Pick a track that is 10 to 15 minutes long. (I especially enjoy tracks by Shamanic Experience or Sandra Ingerman.) Experiment with two or three and decide which one feels right for you. It is best to listen using headphones or on high volume. Start the track once you have gotten comfortable.

Either lie on a comfortable blanket or sit comfortably with both feet on the ground. Start the track and close your eyes.

Picture yourself in a starting place. Mine is a meadow, but yours might be a beach, a mountain, a forest, or any other place. Always trust what comes to you.

When you have pictured yourself in that place, look around to see if you have any spirit guides with you (commonly animals or other allies, which might include mythical creatures or even plants and trees). Ask your spirit guide to journey with you. Next, look for a way to the upper world. It might be a ladder, stairs, or a beanstalk, or you may simply fly. Again, trust what comes to you.

Now imagine yourself journeying to Venus, the ruler of Taurus. Take note of everything that happens and have a conversation with Venus by asking questions.

How can Venus help you grow in the area of your chart where Venus and/or Taurus are?

How can Venus and Taurus support you with your personal growth?

Venus might respond by suggesting how you can be less stubborn and more open to change in areas of your chart or, alternatively, how you can develop the energies of Venus and Taurus to help you embody them in your chart. Remember, this is a conversation where you are seeking to develop your energies in the best way possible for you.

When the conversation is over, thank Venus and return to your starting place. When you are ready to open your eyes, journal about your experience.

SOUTH NODE IN TAURUS

If you have the South Node in Taurus, you are learning to release the instinctive soul habit of attachment to people, places, and things that are no longer helping you evolve in this lifetime. In your instinctual need for security, you often find it difficult to give up any control over financial dealings or your own ability to create wealth, and you are attached to how things have always been rather than being able to see possibilities. As the South Node habits are so instinctual, they often display the more unconscious or unaware traits of the sign.

NORTH NODE IN TAURUS

If you have the North Node in Taurus, you are looking to become more present and to embrace the material world and the world of work. Your evolutionary impulse is to become grounded in reality and more self-sufficient and less dependent on others.

TAURUS THROUGH THE HOUSES

The house where Taurus falls in your natal chart brings deeper insights into those areas of life in which you are making things real, tangible, and sustainable. This is where you naturally create abundance. Bring your awareness to how you might be rigid and opposed to change.

TAURUS IN THE FIRST HOUSE

If you have Taurus in the first house or on the cusp, you are primarily concerned with how people see you and the world you have created. You present yourself to others as stable, practical, unassuming, and patient. To others, you will seem passive and stubborn at times because you respond more to coaxing than being pushed. Awareness of when you are resisting only because you feel pushed may help you distinguish between choosing not to do something and resisting it because you don't like to be pushed.

TAURUS IN THE SECOND HOUSE

Taurus is the natural ruler of the second house, and Taurus in or on the cusp of the second house gives you a strong desire to live in material comfort. You are likely to be very good at creating money. However, the second house and Taurus are also the home of core values, and becoming clear about what those values are for you will help you avoid getting overly attached to material wealth.

TAURUS IN THE THIRD HOUSE

If you have Taurus in or on the cusp of the third house, you think before you speak and mull things over very carefully. You are excellent in negotiations and anything that requires careful thought because you won't be pushed into snap judgments. The downside can be that you may be rigid and have trouble really listening to other views, so developing an ability to be open to other people's perceptions is useful.

TAURUS IN THE FOURTH HOUSE

If you have Taurus in or on the cusp of the fourth house, home and family are important to you, and you need a secure and comfortable home that contains your favorite possessions. Your home is usually quite large with lots of space that connects you with nature. As you age, you may become more of a home-body, preferring to spend time in the home as much as possible and creating a peaceful environment to spend time in. The only real downside to this is the attachment to material things rather than realizing that your true home is within. Meditative practices can help you develop the inner life that provides true security.

TAURUS IN THE FIFTH HOUSE

Taurus in or on the cusp of the fifth house has a great appreciation for beauty and can often be very creative, especially in anything that involves creating something tangible. In love, you need affection, and you are happiest with someone who is devoted to you. You have great pride in any children you have but may almost see them as another "possession"; you may struggle to understand them if they choose a different life path than you would have chosen for them. It would be helpful to learn to see others as individuals rather than as something that belongs to you.

TAURUS IN THE SIXTH HOUSE

If you have Taurus in or on the cusp of the sixth house, you are a hard and reliable worker who owns your worth and value by making sure you are paid well. There may be a tendency to be all about this side of work, however, and neglect the altruistic side of service as you constantly seek recognition for what you are paid to do. You will feel best when you find the right kind of work that fills your senses and aligns with your values.

TAURUS IN THE SEVENTH HOUSE

If you have Taurus in or on the cusp of the seventh house, you are typically attracted to a partner or significant other who brings loyalty, stability, and security into your life—or you bring this to the relationship. There can be a tendency either to see those you are in relationship with as possessions or to be attracted to possessive people. Developing an awareness that true stability comes from within is useful either way.

TAURUS IN THE EIGHTH HOUSE

If you have Taurus in or on the cusp of the eighth house, you are likely to experience material gain through those you are closely bonded with, and you are probably okay with that. On a soul level, Taurus here is apt to doggedly search for truths that have been hidden and to delve deeply into subconscious and psychological realms. Be wary of doing this only to validate your views and be open to new findings.

TAURUS IN THE NINTH HOUSE

If you have Taurus in or on the cusp of the ninth house, you tend to be a traditionalist in concepts of the higher mind, philosophy, truth, and freedom. You stick with what you know and are comfortable with and are likely, for example, to stay in the religion you were brought up in or take a traditional path of education. The challenge is avoiding dogmatic tendencies or imposing your beliefs on others. Instead, try to seek divine personal experiences rather dwell on the outer trappings of faith.

TAURUS IN THE TENTH HOUSE

Taurus in or on the cusp of the tenth house indicates that your public reputation is concerned with how successful you are materially. You are likely to be driven by status and wealth rather than by how much you are helping others. Yet you are charming, and, if you can release the grip of accumulating possessions, you can be successful spiritually as well as materially.

TAURUS IN THE ELEVENTH HOUSE

If you have Taurus in or on the cusp of the eleventh house, you like smaller groups of friends and are very loyal to those groups you are part of. You may have a tendency to try to impress these groups with what you have in life or to attract those who have wealth. You would fit in well with groups that get involved in fundraising for humanitarian causes, and the focus on those pursuits would negate any tendency toward over self-indulgence.

TAURUS IN THE TWELFTH HOUSE

As Taurus is all about self-worth and value, those with Taurus in or on the cusp of the twelfth house, the house of the collective unconscious and connection to the muse and mystery, often find the fluidity of this area difficult, as they like solidity. You might have a tendency to be attracted to prestige and glamour. There's a passive quality to both Taurus and the twelfth house, and awareness of that can help you choose to seek out activities and places that help others so that there is spiritual meaning for you beyond your own self.

TAURUS CASE STUDY

Bill has the following placements in his chart:

- Sun in Taurus in the twelfth house
- Moon in Leo in the second house
- Gemini Ascendant

In this example, we are looking only at the Sun, Moon, and Ascendant, but the case study in Appendix A on page 213 integrates other elements in the natal chart.

Though Bill is very sociable and enjoys company, he often finds that he is exhausted by them, which is common for someone with a twelfth house Sun. Through his work with his natal chart, Bill identifies himself as a silent spirit (Sun in the twelfth house) who is emotionally inclined to be a performer (Leo Moon) and has the persona of someone who is a storyteller. With a Leo Moon in the second house and Gemini Ascendant, Bill's passive and quiet twelfth house Sun is tempered by the more outgoing Moon and Ascendant.

His chart suggests that he needs times when he is in social environments and/or on show, but that he should also schedule alone or retreat time rather than feeling like he must be out and about at all times.

THE SOUL IN TAURUS

The personality and behavior of Taurus, or any Sun sign, is affected by all the other placements and aspects in the natal chart. This is why it is important to gradually blend the meanings of the planets, signs, houses, aspects, and transits to create an overall picture of the potential in your personal blueprint.

If Taurus is your Sun sign, you may have things in common with other Taurus Sun signs, but you are uniquely you. For example, a Taurus Sun with Sagittarius Ascendant will be a lot more outgoing and flexible than a Taurus Sun with Scorpio Ascendant, who would appear to be deeply private and unyielding. Another example is a person with a Taurus Sun and Libra Moon, who would be more highly creative than a person with a Taurus Sun and Virgo Moon, who would be more inclined to routine and daily work.

Here a few things to consider to help you make the most of your Taurus energy in different areas of life. Always consider that your soul chose Taurus energy so that you could be more deliberate, reliable, and solid in that area of life. You can choose to maximize the positive energies of Taurus.

GENERAL PERSONAL DEVELOPMENT

One issue that causes the most problems for Taurus is their tendency to be stubborn and possessive. Of course, sometimes this is a good thing as Taurus is learning to focus on their own needs. However, learning to balance your own needs with those of others helps loosen the grip of this energy.

RELATIONSHIPS/RELATING TO OTHERS

Looking opposite to Taurus, we see Scorpio, the sign of deep intuition, passion, and emotional intensity. Learning to trust your intuition and allow a deeper emotional connection and bonding will help you have more fulfilling relationships. This isn't to suggest that you should become completely like Scorpio—only that you should infuse some of these qualities in your dealings with others in order to have more successful relationships.

ACHIEVING GOALS

Taurus is excellent at making things real and achieving goals. It's their rigidity that makes things more difficult because they find it hard to shift gears or direction. To help with this, look to where Mercury is in your chart (Mercury represents the mind) to see how to shift your thinking. For example, if Mercury is in the third house, you may be able to open your mind to new ideas through a fact-finding exercise, or if Mercury is in the seventh house, you benefit by bouncing ideas off others.

CAREERS

For a full analysis of what type of career you would be suited to, take into account the cusp of the tenth house (the Midheaven), the ruler of that sign, and any planets in the tenth house. For example, a person with a Taurus Sun may have Aquarius on the cusp of the tenth house, and Uranus (ruler of the eleventh house) in the eleventh house, and Neptune in the tenth house. This person might look to more technological areas for their career and could also be drawn to humanitarian careers that, for example, create technological solutions to environmental issues. Or perhaps this person would be drawn to research for natural health cures.

CHAPTER FIVE

gemini the twins

Change what you see, by changing how you see. —JONATHAN LOCKWOOD HUIE

Dates: May 20–June 20, depending on the year

ELEMENT	MODALITY	RULING PLANET	HOUSE RULED
Air	Mutable	Mercury	Third

Gemini is a mutable Air sign and is ruled by Mercury. In this third sign in the zodiac, we start to become aware of consciousness and both our separation from and our connection to others and the world.

Gemini is represented by the Twins. Notice that the glyph for Gemini is two upright lines that are both separate and connected at the top and bottom. Twins are a universal motif that have appeared in myths and legends of all cultures. They represent the mystery of sameness and difference, often depicted sharing a deep bond or fierce rivalry. Notable mythological twins include Apollo and Artemis. In Greek mythology, these twins were the Sun God and Moon Goddess, representing the dualistic nature of the universe. In Egyptian mythology, the Earth God Geb and the Sky Goddess Nut were twins. In some African traditions, the deity is a set of twins, one male and one female.

Gemini represents duality (seeing both or all sides). Gemini is constantly thinking about and *perceiving* the world around them—so much so that this is probably the sign that has the hardest time focusing and concentrating. Gemini is the definition of "shiny object syndrome," constantly distracted by new information as their computer-like brain takes in new information to be analyzed.

Gemini is always active and flitting from one thing to another, endlessly curious about everything. Often eloquent, quick-witted, and highly sociable, their ability to see all sides makes them the shape-shifters of the zodiac. Ruled by Mercury, they are the epitome of the word *mercurial*, subject to sudden or unpredictable changes of mood or mind. For example, someone who has their Sun in Gemini in the fourth house might have a very busy and active home life and a fluctuating home environment, whereas Sun in Gemini in the tenth house needs a career with a lot of variety, probably involving research and/or teaching.

In an unaware state, Gemini energy can twist information and facts to mean anything they choose. This constant inner and outer debate can be hard on the nervous system and can lead to emotional and physical exhaustion. With awareness, Gemini can recognize this tendency and choose to look for the deeper truth.

Now that you have a general feel for Gemini energy, we'll look at *how* the planets show up in Gemini and the houses. With your chart in hand, look for *which* planets you have in Gemini, *how* the planets work in that sign, and *where* in the chart they are—the house. Then you will blend the energies by identifying keywords and phrases from all three that have meaning for you, remembering that you can replace them with any synonyms or phrases with the same meaning of your choosing. With this list, you will create a coherent and meaningful picture to get a deep understanding of how Gemini energy manifests within you. This is where the real awareness and choice comes in. Armed with this knowledge, you can choose how you respond and react to Gemini energy and how you manifest it in the world.

PLANETS IN GEMINI

This section gives you a brief description of each planet in the sign Gemini. I encourage you not to treat these discussions as definitive descriptions, but as a springboard for your own interpretation using similar words and themes. You are invited to use these descriptions and the exercises in this chapter to create your own description of how the energy of Gemini and the planets show up within you.

MOON IN GEMINI

The Moon represents your emotional body, and in Gemini, the emotions are erratic. However, this Moon sign is charming, witty, and loyal to a fault once they have made up their mind about how they feel about someone. The Moon is a receptive energy, and therefore Gemini Moons are likely to react by imitating or by saying what they think is wanted rather than thinking things through. If you have a Gemini Moon, you are interesting and lively company, but be aware that your moodiness and irritable behavior can be off-putting to some people.

MERCURY IN GEMINI

Mercury represents communication and thought processes, and in Gemini, one of the signs that Mercury rules is that both run at full speed. If you have this placement, you are a lifelong learner and endlessly curious. You talk fast and inundate people with information because you are excited to teach others about everything you have taken in. You may also be prone to playing mind games with people, especially if you become in any way bored, considering this active placement. You need a creative channel or to begin studying something new.

VENUS IN GEMINI

Venus represents love, relationships, pleasure, creativity, and the value we place on the material things in life and our own pleasure. Venus in Gemini loves lighthearted, intellectual stimulation in all these areas and will often be found flirting in a very sociable and fun way. There is a lightness that comes with Venus in Gemini, but their constant need for fun and stimulation can mean they move on quickly if relationships no longer provide that. Keep in mind that not all of your important relationships can always be fun and stimulating.

MARS IN GEMINI

Mars represents your will, your drive, and your energy. In Gemini, these energies are somewhat hyperactive and fast-moving and can result in very sharp words. This placement dislikes routine and loves to be in high-energy, high-pressure situations. One of the keywords for Mars is "challenge," and if you have this placement, you will need to be challenged mentally to stay interested. If you aren't challenged, you will either move into aggressive mode or leave. You will more than likely juggle many things at once—jobs, hobbies, and relationships. Be aware that this can lead to none of them having your full attention.

JUPITER IN GEMINI

Jupiter represents expansion, faith, truth, and freedom but also grandiosity. Jupiter in Gemini is all about *more*. This placement makes prolific writers and teachers who are often very gifted linguistically. If you have this placement, you are likely to be curious about other cultures and religions and will explore them either physically or mentally. You are also a natural philosopher, exploring all kinds of philosophy—from religion to ethics and beyond. Because you have endless energy for exploration and are a multitasker, you are also exhausting to be around and may forget to keep pace with other people. Your biggest "issue" is fitting it all in because you don't want to miss a thing.

SATURN IN GEMINI

Saturn represents mastery, determination, and discipline. Saturn in Gemini does a lot to ground this energy and focus the multitude of ideas that are constantly moving through your mind. The shadow of Saturn is fear, and this can cause Gemini to feel restricted, especially when they are younger. They may be reluctant to express the myriad ideas they have inside for fear of not being enough. If you have this placement, once you understand that Saturn's strength is grounding and bringing focus to your thoughts and ideas in a way that helps you communicate clearly and succinctly, you will be able to move beyond these fears.

URANUS IN GEMINI

Uranus represents individuality, unpredictability, and unconventionality. If you have Uranus in Gemini, you have the potential for genius energy. Inventive, original, and somewhat eccentric, you may shock others with your ideas. Usually hugely progressive and broad-minded, people with Uranus in Gemini can be forerunners in any field they love. Often they love science, astrology, the Internet, and other analytical subjects that expand their mind.

NEPTUNE IN GEMINI

Neptune represents inspiration, illusion, psychic sensitivity, healing, and confusion. Neptune in Gemini has a visionary mind but can often live in illusion and idealize the world around them. Both Neptune and Gemini are shape-shifting energies, so this placement is restless and even more unfocused than most other planets in Gemini. The world may seem magical if you have this placement, but be wary of those who might want to deceive you.

PLUTO IN GEMINI

Pluto is the soul or the soul's desire. Pluto spends approximately 20 years in each sign, so the mighty dwarf planet's influence is generational, which means that everyone in a generation is influenced by the sign that Pluto is in. The house placement must be blended with the generational concepts to get a clear picture for your own cosmic blueprint.

Pluto was in Gemini from 1884 to 1914 and will return in 2132. Those born with Pluto in Gemini were and will be interested in the hidden realms and can be drawn to deep exploration of people's deep psychological motivations, death, and other taboo subjects. Mother Teresa, Alfred Hitchcock, and Al Capone were all born with Pluto in Gemini.

SOUTH NODE IN GEMINI

If you have the South Node in Gemini, you are learning to release the instinctive soul habit of mental insecurity. Your perpetual need for information and trying to figure out what others are thinking is so instinctual that it holds you back from true connection. "One more book, one more class" could be your mantra. The evolutionary impulse for this placement is to begin to trust what you already know and speak from your inner wisdom.

NORTH NODE IN GEMINI

If you have the North Node in Gemini, you are looking to develop a healthy sense of curiosity, an openness to new information, and changing your perceptions about the world. Your evolutionary impulse is to develop listening skills and to realize that you are not always right.

Shamanic Journey to Mercury, Ruler of Gemini

In this exercise you are going to journey to non-ordinary reality, the upper world, in a practice called shamanic journey work. This is similar to a meditation but enables you to actively ask for guidance and answers. Shamanic journey work is an amazing practice for getting support in life. You can take a shamanic journey as often as you would like.

For this journey, search the term "Shamanic Drumming" on YouTube or your preferred video-streaming platform. Pick a track that is 10 to 15 minutes long. (I especially enjoy tracks by Shamanic Experience or Sandra Ingerman.) Experiment with two or three and decide which one feels right for you. It is best to listen using headphones or on high volume. Start the track once you have gotten comfortable.

Either lie on a comfortable blanket or sit comfortably with both feet on the ground. Start the track and close your eyes.

Picture yourself in a starting place. Mine is a meadow, but yours might be a beach, a mountain, a forest or any other place. Always trust what comes to you.

When you have pictured yourself in that place, look around to see if you have any spirit guides (commonly animals or other allies, which might include mythical creatures or even plants and trees). Ask your spirit guide(s) to journey with you. Next, look for a way to the upper world. It might be a ladder, stairs, or a beanstalk, or you may simply fly. Again, trust what comes to you.

Now imagine yourself journeying to Mercury, the ruler of Gemini. Take note of everything that happens and have a conversation with Mercury by asking questions.

How can Mercury help you grow in the area of your chart where Mercury and/or Gemini are?

How can Mercury and Gemini support you with your personal growth?

Mercury might respond by suggesting how you can be more open and curious or, alternatively, how you can develop the energies of Mercury and Gemini to help you embody them in your chart. Remember, this is a conversation where you are seeking to develop your energies in the best way possible for you.

When the conversation is over, thank Mercury and return to your starting place. When you are ready to open your eyes, journal about your experience.

GEMINI THROUGH THE HOUSES

The house where Gemini falls in your natal chart brings deeper insights into those areas of life in which you are learning, taking in information, and communicating. This is where you are naturally curious. Bring your awareness to how you might never be satisfied with the amount of information you have taken in.

GEMINI IN THE FIRST HOUSE

If you have Gemini in or on the cusp of the first house, you are sociable and friendly and strike up conversations with everyone you meet. You are seen as intellectual and adaptable. The conversations you strike up are wide-ranging, but don't always have depth. Because you are so adaptable, you can at times be seen as shallow and somewhat fickle. But overall you are seen as a lot of fun to be around.

GEMINI IN THE SECOND HOUSE

If you have Gemini in or on the cusp of the second house, you can make money through anything related to communication, such as writing, journalism, or teaching. You also take a cerebral approach to your finances and are likely to be excellent at creating budgets and financial plans. It would be useful to remember that money is an expression of value in the material world rather than just numbers on paper. Money supports daily living. It is a useful practice for you to consciously connect it to your physical life and what the money has provided rather than constantly planning and budgeting.

GEMINI IN THE THIRD HOUSE

Gemini is the natural ruler of the third house, so if you have Gemini in or on the cusp of the third house, you are a master communicator and a fast learner with an extremely quick mind that needs constant mental stimulation. You are able to handle a great amount of detail and are very open to new ideas. Your need for details, activity, and stimulation makes it difficult for you to step back and see the bigger picture at times.

GEMINI IN THE FOURTH HOUSE

If you have Gemini in or on the cusp of the fourth house, you have a very busy home life with lots of comings and goings but little real bonding and connection. Similarly, your inner life is mentally active as you use your mind to try to connect with your receptive, feeling self. Learn to release the need to try to make sense of things and just feel.

GEMINI IN THE FIFTH HOUSE

Gemini in or on the cusp of the fifth house prefers mental creativity, such as writing, and also prefers a lot of variety. You are also likely to stimulate the intellectual potential of any children you have or are acquainted with. You also prefer love and life to be fun and light. The fifth house is ruled by Leo, making it a Fire house, and because Gemini is an Air sign, the air fans the flames of the fire to bring a more joyful vibe to situations. However, be aware that, at times, that vibe can be rash or appear fickle as you hop from activity to activity.

GEMINI IN THE SIXTH HOUSE

If you have Gemini in or on the cusp of the sixth house, you prefer a fast-paced and varied work environment, and one that also requires you to use your mental and communication abilities. You may even choose to work more than one job at a time. As both the sixth house and Gemini are ruled by Mercury, this can create a nerve-racking energy that can impact your health if you don't learn to calm yourself. Breathing exercises are useful here.

GEMINI IN THE SEVENTH HOUSE

Gemini in or on the cusp of the seventh house indicates that you are attracted to a partner or significant other at an intellectual level. You need to be around people who stimulate your mind and who have varied interests. You may also enjoy being around people who are younger than you, and you may even have a younger life partner or, at least, one who has a youthful outlook. If a relationship doesn't provide that intellectual stimulation, you are likely to move on.

GEMINI IN THE EIGHTH HOUSE

If you have Gemini in or on the cusp of the eighth house, you take an intellectual approach to joint finances, and you are full of investment and other financial ideas. As this is also the house of the deep psyche and the metaphysical, you also take an investigative, intellectual approach to these matters, but it is helpful to remember that these are areas that cannot always be rationalized and reasoned and must be delved into in a deeper way. Any practice that helps you connect at an emotional level, such as shamanic journey work, will help you work with the energies of this house at a more satisfactory level.

GEMINI IN THE NINTH HOUSE

Those with Gemini in or on the cusp of the ninth house are the student in the house of the teacher; they have both an avaricious need for knowledge and a need to communicate that knowledge to others. As this is also the house of belief systems, you are likely to analyze the facts of the belief systems you encounter and be quite changeable based on the new information you find. You are also likely to learn through travel.

GEMINI IN THE TENTH HOUSE

Gemini in or on the cusp of the tenth house indicates that you need variety in your career or public role in life, and you are defined by your intellect in this area. As the tenth house is your mission or contribution, more than merely your career, this will involve imparting the vast knowledge you have gained. You are likely to do this in a variety of ways (teaching, writing, or working with young people, for example). However, be aware that you may also have a tendency to spread yourself so thin that people see you as flighty in your work.

GEMINI IN THE ELEVENTH HOUSE

If you have Gemini in or on the cusp of the eleventh house, you have a lot of friends but few close friends. You are probably associated with a few groups so that you can flit between them as you tire of one group or when one group can't keep up with you! You love bouncing ideas off other people, but be wary of your tendency to shape-shift and take on the ideas of others in the group as if they were your own or shifting your own ideas to fit in.

GEMINI IN THE TWELFTH HOUSE

As Gemini is all about perception and communication, if you have Gemini in or on the cusp of the twelfth house, the house of the collective unconscious and connection to the muse and mystery, you tend to attract secrets and can take in information from the unconscious and teach it to others. This house is ruled by Pisces, a Water sign, and the watery mysteries of the twelfth house add a compassionate dimension to the active Gemini mind that isn't always evident in other houses.

GEMINI CASE STUDY

June has the following placements in her chart:

- Sun in Gemini in the seventh house
- Moon in Cancer in the eighth house
- Scorpio Ascendant

In this example, we are looking only at the Sun, Moon, and Ascendant, but the case study in Appendix A on page 213 integrates other elements in the natal chart.

June has very deep and strong emotions, while her core self, Gemini Sun, likes to rationalize everything. She struggles to understand why she can't always do that with her emotions. Through her work with her natal chart, June identifies herself as a storyteller lover (Sun in the seventh house) who is emotionally inclined to be a deep healer (Cancer Moon in the eighth house) and has the persona of someone who is a magician. With a Cancer Moon in the eighth house and Scorpio Ascendant, her airy and sociable seventh house Sun is given a deeply emotional, intuitive, and private side by the Cancer Moon in the house ruled by Scorpio and the Scorpio Ascendant.

June's chart helps her understand how she needs to give herself permission to withdraw from her constant need to tell stories and to learn and allow time for meditation, contemplation, and privacy so that her active Gemini core doesn't ignore or override her deep emotions.

Gemini Strategies to Improve Intuitive Skills

Gemini often find it difficult to tap into their intuitive or gut feelings because they are so "of the mind." The following strategies will help you calm your mental activity and tune in to your intuitive abilities.

1. Develop a meditation or shamanic journey work practice to calm your over-active mind. Either a walking meditation or active meditation such as journey work would be more effective than sitting in meditation, because these activities do not try to empty the mind but rather activate the part of the mind that is connected to the intuition. This practice will be most effective if you do it daily, but try to practice a minimum of three times a week.

2. Every morning upon waking, pick up a pen and paper and write up to three pages of stream-of-consciousness writing, allowing all your thoughts to flow onto the page without editing yourself. You don't even need to use full sentences or punctuation. This practice is called "Morning Pages," and to quote Julia Cameron, the author of *The Artist's Way* (who popularized the term and the practice), this activity will "provoke, clarify, comfort, cajole, prioritize and synchronize the day at hand." This helps you tap in to your deep psyche.

3. Be mindful of when you are stepping into shape-shifter mode or agreeing with all sides. Pause, and ask yourself, "What is true for me?" Check in with your gut to feel your truth and make your suggestions and decisions based on that.

THE SOUL IN GEMINI

The personality and behavior of Gemini, or any Sun sign, is affected by all the other placements and aspects in the natal chart. This is why it is important to gradually blend the meanings of the planets, signs, houses, aspects, and transits to create an overall picture of the potential in your personal blueprint.

If Gemini is your Sun sign, you may have things in common with other Gemini Sun signs, but you are uniquely you. For example, a Gemini Sun with Sagittarius Ascendant will be very flexible, fun, and outgoing compared to a Gemini Sun with Capricorn Ascendant, who will be more serious and probably a leader in their field. Another example is a person with a Gemini Sun and Aquarius Moon, who would be highly inventive but very detached emotionally, compared with a person with a Gemini Sun and Pisces Moon, who would be more connected to subconscious messages and be more empathic.

Here are a few things to consider to help you make the most of your Gemini energy in different areas of life. Always consider that your soul chose the Gemini energy so that you could be more of a thinker and teacher in that area of life. You can choose to maximize the positive energies of Gemini.

GENERAL PERSONAL DEVELOPMENT

One issue that causes the most problems for Gemini is their tendency to be unfocused and sometimes unaware of other people's feelings, as well as their own. Of course, sometimes this is a good thing as Gemini's path is to learn as much as they can in this lifetime. However, balancing out the desire to absorb information with focusing on what is true for you is a useful skill to develop.

RELATIONSHIPS/RELATING TO OTHERS

Gemini is the opposite sign of Sagittarius, the sign of the teacher. This means it can be good for Gemini to actually teach as well as take in information. This isn't to suggest that you should become completely like Sagittarius—only that you should infuse some of these qualities in your dealings with others to have more successful relationships.

Mercury and Gemini Journaling Exercise

Choose a quiet time and place to look at your natal chart and have your journal handy. Identify Mercury and Gemini in your chart. Look at the sign placement of Mercury and the house placement of both Mercury and Gemini. You can look at Gemini in the houses (see page 67) to get a feel for what Mercury in the houses may also mean.

In your journal, write down keywords and phrases from this book and from your shamanic journey to Mercury. Reflect on how you manifest these energies in your life and how you might choose to develop these energies in a more conscious rather than reactive way. For example, you may have Mercury or Gemini in the second house and realize that you are in a line of work that doesn't fully utilize your mental abilities. Through this awareness, you might choose to work toward a position that is better suited for you and in which you might find more success. Record your reflections in your journal.

Through this journaling exercise and your shamanic journey to Mercury, you will begin to really understand the energies in your chart. Through that awareness, you will be able to choose *how* you embody the energies of Mercury and Gemini in your life.

ACHIEVING GOALS

Gemini loses interest in things quickly and moves on to new things, which can make achieving a goal difficult. It's Gemini's changeability that results in things being more arduous for them. To help you with this, look to where Saturn is in your chart to discover how you can tap in to the energy of mastery before you move on to something new.

CAREERS

For a full analysis of what type of career you would be suited to, take into account the cusp of the tenth house (the Midheaven), the ruler of that sign, and any planets in the tenth house. For example, a person with a Gemini Sun may have Virgo on the cusp of the tenth house, and Mercury (ruler of both Gemini and Virgo) in the eighth house in Cancer. This person might be drawn to studying healing and metaphysics, and they may even become a teacher of such practices.

CHAPTER SIX

cancer the crab

Bran thought about it. "Can a man still be brave if he's afraid?" "That is the only time a man can be brave," his father told him. —GEORGE R.R. MARTIN, *A GAME OF THRONES*

Dates: June 20–July 20, depending on the year

ELEMENT	MODALITY	RULING PLANET	HOUSE RULED
Water	Cardinal	The Moon	Fourth

Cancer is a cardinal Water sign and is ruled by the Moon. It's the fourth sign in the zodiac and is where we begin to become aware of our inner life and our own emotions.

Cancer is represented by the Crab. Notice that the glyph for Cancer is often described as two fishes, but is actually the Crab's claws closed in and holding on to things. This in itself gives you a clue about the nature of this sign. The Crab moves in a sideways motion and has a protective shell that it retreats into when threatened to ensure the safety of its soft inner parts. Its claws hold on tight to anything in its grasp, and it doesn't let go easily.

Already we are getting a feel for Cancer's protective, nurturing, and soft energy. Ruled by the Moon, we can look at the Moon itself to understand Cancer energy more deeply. The Moon rules the movement of water on earth and also the physical cycles of women in their fertile years. That's why it is associated with mothering energy.

The Moon is a receptive luminary and emanates no light itself. It also has no atmosphere, so anything that affects its surface stays forever. This is reflected in the energy of Cancer and its ruler, as Cancer has a long memory and soaks up external energies like a sponge. This means that Cancer is extremely empathic, sensitive, and responsive. The Moon also has phases and the fastest cycle of all our planetary energies, which is reflected in the moodiness of Cancer energy.

Cancer is a Water sign, and water in shamanic terms represents our emotions, and the Moon is our emotional body, making this sign the most emotional of the zodiac. To Cancer, everything is feeling. They are also natural healers. For example, the Sun in Cancer in the tenth house might mean that this person's mission in life is to heal and nurture, or if the Sun is in Cancer in the first house, others will see this person as nurturing.

When unaware, Cancer energy can be very emotionally needy and moody as they look to others to fulfill their emotional needs. With awareness, Cancer can choose to look to themselves for this fulfillment.

Now that you have a general feel for Cancer energy, we'll look at *how* the planets show up in Cancer and the houses. With your chart in hand, look for *which* planets you have in Cancer, *how* the planets work in that sign, and *where* in the chart they are—the house. Then you will blend the energies by identifying keywords and phrases from all three that have meaning for you, remembering that you can replace them with any synonyms or phrases with the same meaning of your choosing. With this list, you will create a coherent and meaningful picture to get a deep understanding of how Cancer energy manifests within you. This is where the real awareness and choice comes in. Armed with this knowledge, you can choose how you respond and react to Cancer energy and how you manifest it in the world.

PLANETS IN CANCER

This section gives you a brief description of each planet in the sign Cancer. I encourage you not to treat these discussions as definitive descriptions but as a springboard for your own interpretation using similar words and themes. You are invited to use these descriptions and the exercises in this chapter to create your own description of how the energy of Cancer and the planets show up within you.

MOON IN CANCER

The Moon represents your emotional body, and in Cancer, the sign that it rules, everything is heightened. These people are extra sensitive, extra emotional, and extra nurturing. They *never* forget, and their powerful memories can be used to weave emotion into their creativity and stories so that they pull at the memories of others. If you have Moon in Cancer, you are deeply affectionate and loving to anyone you are in a relationship with, but remain aware that you can also be easily hurt and react by being critical and clingy.

MERCURY IN CANCER

Mercury represents communication and thought processes, and in Cancer, both thought and communication have sensitive, subtle, and instinctual qualities. Mercury in Cancer processes information according to their feelings about it and, therefore, can seem slow to respond as they process information internally. Similarly, they are often slow to speak and can seem very shy and/or thoughtful, which they are. If you have this placement, you naturally always feel before you speak.

VENUS IN CANCER

Venus represents love, relationships, pleasure, creativity, and the value we place on the material things in life and our own pleasure. This is a very creative placement, and Venus in Cancer loves a harmonious and beautiful environment. If you have Venus in Cancer, you are cautious in relationships due to your sensitive nature and the real possibility of getting deeply hurt. Once hurt, you retreat, but with the right person, however, you are nurturing and deeply loving.

MARS IN CANCER

Mars represents your will, your drive, and your energy. In Cancer, your will is ruled by your emotions, and you feel your way into doing things. You are likely to hang back or circle around, testing the waters until you get a feel for when the right moment is to leap into action. This placement never fakes interest; their heart has to be in it. If you sense conflict, you withdraw quickly into your shell.

JUPITER IN CANCER

Jupiter represents expansion, faith, truth, and freedom but also grandiosity. Jupiter in Cancer is all about more feelings, more faith, and more moodiness. Their compassion is endless and their generosity great. These are beautiful, intuitive qualities, but they can open you up to an even bigger need for security and a safe home space as you literally feel the needs of the world in a big way. With this placement, you are also quite conventional, so be aware of not being open to trying new things.

SATURN IN CANCER

Saturn represents mastery, determination, and discipline. Saturn in Cancer is reserved about demonstrating their emotions, preferring to hide their feelings for fear of not seeming strong. Their family is of extreme importance as Saturn in Cancer is, in effect, both mother and father to others. Their huge sense of emotional responsibility for others makes it difficult, however, to receive love in return. If you have Saturn in Cancer, learn to move past any fears of not being or doing enough for others and be open to receive.

URANUS IN CANCER

Uranus represents individuality, unpredictability, and unconventionality. If you have Uranus in Cancer, you are likely to be highly sensitive to erratic energies and may experience a lot of emotional ups and downs. You are very intuitive and creatively inventive and are likely to somehow "break the mold" in the home.

NEPTUNE IN CANCER

Neptune represents inspiration, illusion, psychic sensitivity, healing, and confusion. Neptune in Cancer is deeply sensitive and intuitive and loves to have a beautiful home. If you have this placement, be aware that you may have a tendency to idealize your home and family. You may feel deep loss and disappointment if things don't live up to your dreams.

PLUTO IN CANCER

Pluto is the soul or the soul's desire. Pluto spends approximately 20 years in each sign, so the mighty dwarf planet's influence is generational, which means that everyone in a generation is influenced by the sign that Pluto is in. The house placement must be blended with the generational concepts to get a clear picture for your own natal cosmic blueprint.

Pluto was in Cancer from 1914 to 1939 and will return in 2159. Those born with Pluto in Cancer were and will be emotionally intense and can be overwhelming to those around them. This is a deeply healing placement, however, as this person is not afraid to face complex emotional issues. Marilyn Monroe, Martin Luther King, Jr., John F. Kennedy, and Elvis Presley were all born with Pluto in Cancer.

SOUTH NODE IN CANCER

If you have the South Node in Cancer, you are learning to release the instinctive soul habits of emotional dependence and insecurity. You are born needing others to take care of your emotional needs, and that can lead you to constantly seek security from others. You can also have a tendency to be emotionally manipulative as your fears lead the way.

NORTH NODE IN CANCER

If you have the North Node in Cancer, you are learning to get in touch with your own emotions and empathic nature and how to express those emotions. You are also learning to allow others to take charge of their own lives rather than trying to control them.

CANCER THROUGH THE HOUSES

The house where Cancer falls in your natal chart brings deeper insights into those areas of life in which you are emotional and intuitive. This is where you are naturally creative and nurturing. Bring your awareness to how you might also be emotionally needy or moody in this area.

Shamanic Journey to the Moon, Ruler of Cancer

In this exercise, you are going to journey to non-ordinary reality, the upper world, in a practice called shamanic journey work. This is similar to a meditation but enables you to actively ask for guidance and answers. Shamanic journey work is an amazing practice for getting support in life. You can take a shamanic journey as often as you would like.

For this journey, search the term "Shamanic Drumming" on YouTube or your preferred video-streaming platform. Pick a track that is 10 to 15 minutes long. (I especially enjoy tracks by Shamanic Experience or Sandra Ingerman.) Experiment with two or three and decide which one feels right for you. It is best to listen using headphones or on high volume. Start the track once you have gotten comfortable.

Either lie on a comfortable blanket or sit comfortably with both feet on the ground. Start the track and close your eyes.

Picture yourself in a starting place. Mine is a meadow, but yours might be a beach, a mountain, a forest or any other place. Always trust what comes to you.

When you have pictured yourself in that place, look around to see if you have any spirit guides with you (commonly animals or other allies, which might include mythical creatures or even plants and trees). Ask your spirit guide(s) to journey with you. Next, look for a way to the upper world. It might be a ladder, stairs, or a beanstalk, or you may simply fly. Again, trust what comes to you.

Now imagine yourself journeying to the Moon, the ruler of Cancer. Take note of everything that happens and have a conversation with the Moon by asking questions.

How can the Moon help you grow in the area of your chart where the Moon and/or Cancer are?

How can the Moon and Cancer support you with your personal growth?

The Moon might respond by suggesting how you can express your emotions without falling into neediness or, alternatively, how you can develop the nurturing and empathic energies of Cancer and embody them in your chart. Remember, this is a conversation where you are seeking to develop your energies in the best way possible for you.

When the conversation is over, thank the Moon and return to your starting place. When you are ready to open your eyes, journal your experience.

CANCER IN THE FIRST HOUSE

If you have Cancer in or on the cusp of the first house, you are seen as a nurturing and motherly person, regardless of gender, and someone who takes care of those around them. Because this is how people meet you one-on-one, you are also meeting others one-on-one and will pick up their emotions, which often makes you protective and shy at first as you are reluctant to allow others into your "home" until you get to know them.

CANCER IN THE SECOND HOUSE

If you have Cancer in or on the cusp of the second house, your emotional security is tied into your material security. You'll probably feel particularly unsafe if your financial security is ever threatened. This does mean that you are likely to save and invest wisely. You are also inclined to find ways to make your nurturing activities and healing modalities profitable.

CANCER IN THE THIRD HOUSE

If you have Cancer in or on the cusp of the third house, you learn through connecting to how you feel about information. You have one of the best memories out there, as the information stays stored in your emotions. This means you remember how you felt when you were learning, and that helps your memory retrieval. Be aware, however, that this can lead to a lack of objectivity.

CANCER IN THE FOURTH HOUSE

Cancer is the ruler of the fourth house and is at home here, so if you have Cancer in or on the cusp of the fourth house, you are very oriented around your family and home, and love family gatherings—especially those held where you live. You also enjoy traditions and need to put down roots to feel secure. This is an extremely empathic placement, so be sure to take retreats by yourself to protect yourself from taking on too much of other people's emotions.

CANCER IN THE FIFTH HOUSE

If you have Cancer in or on the cusp of the fifth house, you have a highly creative side that pours emotion into your creations. You are also likely to find deep joy through nurturing any children you have. The love affair side of the house is light, and Cancer doesn't really do light affairs. Your depth of emotion is more suited to your cautious approach to love; "affairs" don't work for you. You are unlikely to have sporting or highly physical hobbies, preferring to cook or engage in other domestic activities.

CANCER IN THE SIXTH HOUSE

If you have Cancer in or on the cusp of the sixth house, you love to help people through your profession. You are likely to be emotionally attached to your work and deeply affected by any ups and downs. If there is any instability in your work, you are physically affected, particularly by stomach issues. You care deeply about the people you work with. You work best in any situation that involves families or mothering/nurturing.

CANCER IN THE SEVENTH HOUSE

Cancer in or on the cusp of the seventh house indicates that you are attracted to a partner or significant other who is sensitive and nurturing. You also need emotional and financial stability to feel secure. You need to both nurture and be nurtured, making your close relationships deeply emotional. Your loyalty is paramount, and you need the same from others.

CANCER IN THE EIGHTH HOUSE

If you have Cancer in or on the cusp of the eighth house, your emotions run deep and can go to dark places at times. There's also a risk of deep dependency on others and allowing yourself to be overpowered emotionally. However, it can also be a place of amazing psychological depth that enables you to heal both the self and others because you are not afraid to hold space for transformation.

CANCER IN THE NINTH HOUSE

If you have Cancer in or on the cusp of the ninth house, you have a tendency to stick to the beliefs of the family you were brought up in; you are generally a traditionalist. You are also emotionally attached to your beliefs and are hurt if they are questioned. You likely enjoy travel with family as well.

CANCER IN THE TENTH HOUSE

Cancer in or on the cusp of the tenth house indicates that you need stability in your career, and your mission in life is to heal and nurture. Those with this placement often stay in the same role for most of their lives because of their emotional attachment and need for security. The better you do financially in this area, the more emotionally secure you are.

CANCER IN THE ELEVENTH HOUSE

If you have Cancer in or on the cusp of the eleventh house, you are likely to have a close group of friends that you keep for a long time. They are like family to you, and you love entertaining these small groups in your home. You are drawn to humanitarian pursuits that help those closer to home or helping families.

CANCER IN THE TWELFTH HOUSE

As Cancer is all about security and emotions, if you have Cancer in or on the cusp of the twelfth house, the house of the collective unconscious and connection to the muse and mystery, you tend to have a powerful emotional connection to the collective and want to heal the world. As both the Cancer sign and the twelfth house are receptive, be aware that this can indicate a lack of boundaries; you will retreat into your shell if you overgive.

CANCER CASE STUDY

Charles has the following placements in his chart:

- Sun in Cancer in the eighth house
- Moon in Aquarius in the third house
- Scorpio Ascendant

In this example, we are looking only at the Sun, Moon, and Ascendant, but the case study in Appendix A on page 213 integrates other elements in the natal chart.

Charles sometimes has difficulties making closely bonded emotional connections with others in his life, and they often describe him as emotionally distant and private. Through his work with his natal chart, Charles identifies himself as a deep healer (Sun in the eighth house) who is emotionally inclined to be a revolutionary voice (Aquarius Moon in the third house) and has the persona of someone who is a magician but who is very private about his emotional life. With an Aquarius Moon in the third house and Scorpio Ascendant, Charles's very watery and emotional eighth house Sun is tempered by the detachment of the third house Aquarius Moon, although the Scorpio Ascendant means he is intense and has a very private inner life.

Charles's chart suggests to him that if he finds strategies to help him connect more deeply and to learn identify, validate, and express his feelings, he will be able to form longer-lasting and more meaningful bonds with others.

THE SOUL IN CANCER

The personality and behavior of Cancer, or any Sun sign, is affected by all the other placements and aspects in the natal chart. This is why it is important to gradually blend the meanings of the planets, signs, houses, aspects, and transits to create an overall picture of the potential in your personal blueprint.

If Cancer is your Sun sign, you may have things in common with other Cancer Sun signs, but you are uniquely you. For example, a Cancer Sun with Pisces Ascendant will be intuitive and creative compared with a Cancer Sun with Aquarius Ascendant who will appear to be emotionally detached and hide their true emotions. Another example is a person with a Cancer Sun and Taurus Moon, who would be a real homebody and needs their comforts and possessions, compared with a person with a Cancer Sun and Aries Moon, who would be more likely to take risks than most others with a Cancer Sun sign.

Here are a few things to consider to help you to make the most of your Cancer energy in different areas of life. Always consider that your soul chose the Cancer energy so that you could be more of a healer and nurturer in that area of life. You can choose to maximize the positive energies of Cancer.

Cancer Strategies to Reduce Emotional Dependence

Cancer is deeply nurturing and protective of those they love, but the shadow of this is emotional dependence that is really caused by fear. These exercises will help you work through this tendency.

1. A simple exercise that can help you be less emotionally dependent and grow your self-worth is the "I am" exercise. Set a timer for one minute. In that minute, write as many "I am" statements as possible. When the timer goes off, review your list and cross out any "role" statements, such as "I am a mom," leaving only descriptive statements, such as "I am kind." You may find this challenging at first, so I suggest repeating the practice periodically to improve your self-esteem and self-awareness. (If you find yourself writing negative statements, such as "I am lazy," turn that into a positive—for example, "I am laid back." If this is difficult, explore the origins of any negative beliefs to realize they are undeserved self-judgments.)

2. Spend time alone to truly get to know yourself. Take yourself on a date once a week for coffee or tea, go for a walk in the park, or visit a gallery. Get to know yourself by taking note of what interests you on your walk, how the beverage tastes, what paintings or artwork draw your attention, and so on. Have a good time paying attention to you!

3. Find an exercise you love to do and do it every day for 30 minutes. Exercise releases endorphins, "feel-good" chemicals, so you just feel better inside. As a result, your self-esteem grows. And while you are starting your exercise routine, make it a habit to eat healthy food. Exercise and healthy eating go hand in hand.

GENERAL PERSONAL DEVELOPMENT

One issue that causes the most problems for Cancer is their tendency to retreat into their shell when they feel insecure. Ironically, sharing their feelings with others helps to actually build the connection that will bring that security. Developing the ability to tell your loved ones what you are feeling will bring the reward of a truly intimate relationship.

RELATIONSHIPS/RELATING TO OTHERS

If we look opposite Cancer we see Capricorn, the sign of authority and a more stoic approach to life, so it is good for Cancer to work on developing a calmer, more grounded approach in their relationships. This isn't to suggest that you should become completely like Capricorn—only that you should infuse some of these qualities in your dealings with others to have more successful relationships.

ACHIEVING GOALS

Cancer tends to limit themselves when trying to achieve their goals because they start clinging to what they have already achieved for fear of losing it. The true goal of Cancer, however, is to find inner security and know that outer trappings never bring true security. Integrating this understanding will help you reach your practical goals and aspire to new ones.

CAREERS

For a full analysis of what type of career you would be suited to, take into account the cusp of the tenth house (the Midheaven), the ruler of that sign, and any planets in the tenth house. For example, a person with a Cancer Sun may have Leo on the cusp of the tenth house, and their Sun (ruler of Leo) in the first house. This person might be drawn to more playful modes of healing, or working with children in a healing capacity.

Moon and Cancer Journaling Exercise

Choose a quiet time and place to look at your natal chart and have your journal handy. Identify the Moon and Cancer in your chart. Look at the sign placement of the Moon and the house placement of both the Moon and Cancer. You can look at Cancer in the houses (see page 79) to get a feel for what the Moon in the houses may also mean.

In your journal, write down keywords and phrases from this book and from your shamanic journey to the Moon. Reflect on how you manifest these energies in your life and how you might choose to develop these energies in a more conscious rather than reactive way. For example, you may have the Moon or Cancer in the third house and realize that you are overly attached to some outdated ideas, such as men always having to make the first move in dating. Through this awareness, you might choose to work toward being more open to change by taking in new information. Record your reflections in your journal.

Through this journaling exercise and your shamanic journey to the Moon, you will begin to really understand the energies in your chart. Through that awareness, you will be able to choose *how* you embody the energies of the Moon and Cancer in your life.

leo
the lion

Love is life. And if you miss love, you miss life. —LEO BUSCAGLIA

Dates: July 20–August 20, depending on the year

ELEMENT	MODALITY	RULING PLANET	HOUSE RULED
Fire	Fixed	The Sun	Fifth

Leo is a fixed Fire sign and is ruled by the Sun. It's the fifth sign in the zodiac and is where we begin to become aware of our creativity and what brings us joy and pleasure.

Leo is represented by the Lion. Notice that the glyph for Leo resembles a mane of hair. The Lion is the most regal animal, and, in astrology, it is generally seen as the masculine, but in shamanism, the Lion is also seen as the assertion of the feminine. In some cultures, the Sun, which is the ruler of Leo, is seen as masculine and feminine, and in other cultures, it is the one or the other.

Lions live in prides. The word *pride* is very representative of Leo. While female lions do the majority of the hunting and child-rearing, the alpha male often does little work. However, it is the alpha male who protects against predators and rules over the pride with passion and often possessiveness. As a pride, lions are affectionate and playful, and the cubs lead a carefree life. The behavior of the pride gives us a feel for Leo energy: playful, regal, dramatic, and passionate. Since Leo is ruled by the Sun, we can look at the Sun itself to understand Leo energy more deeply. The Sun is the center of our solar system, and everything in that system revolves around it. It's the giver of life and shines most brightly.

As a Fire sign, Leo reflects the solar energy. Leo shines brightly and is dynamic, magnetic, and comfortable in the spotlight. They are generous, playful, and charming. At their best, they inspire others with their confident creativity and are loving and kind. For example, a person who has the Sun in Leo in the second house might make money through work that is in the public eye, such as the theater, or if the Sun is in Leo in the eleventh house, such a person is likely to take the lead in groups.

In an unaware state, Leo energy can be very self-absorbed and grandiose, behaving as if they are superior to others. With awareness, Leo can choose to see and treat other people more as equals.

Now that you have a general feel for Leo energy, we'll look at *how* the planets show up in Leo and the houses. With your chart in hand, look for *which* planets you have in Leo, *how* the planets work in that sign, and *where* in the chart they are—the house. Then you will blend the energies by identifying keywords and phrases from all three that have meaning for you, remembering that you can replace them with any synonyms or phrases with the same meaning of your choosing. With this list, you will create a coherent and meaningful picture to get a deep understanding of how Leo energy manifests within you. This is where the real awareness and choice comes in. Armed with this knowledge, you can choose how you respond and react to Leo energy and how you manifest it in the world.

PLANETS IN LEO

This section gives you a brief description of each planet in the sign Leo. I encourage you not to treat these discussions as definitive descriptions but as a springboard for your own interpretation using similar words and themes. You are invited to use these descriptions and the exercises in this chapter to create your own description of how the energy of Leo and the planets show up within you.

MOON IN LEO

The Moon represents your emotional body, and in Leo, this means you are fiery, passionate, highly creative, and playful. You need lots of loving attention and give the same in return. You are, at heart, sensitive and need the approval of others. If you don't receive the attention you need, your fire dies and you feel hurt. There's a real emotional need for creative self-expression with the Moon in Leo, but if you are wary of being emotionally demanding and allow others their own emotional needs, you will receive the love you crave.

MERCURY IN LEO

Mercury represents communication and thought processes, and a person with Mercury in Leo is usually a captivating speaker with dramatic flair that commands attention. The need to express with passion often leads to overlooking details, but these really are the performers and dramatic storytellers who can entertain with humor and heart. If you have this placement, you are warm and generous in social situations—unless the attention is off you.

VENUS IN LEO

Venus represents love, relationships, pleasure, creativity, and the value we place on the material things in life and our pleasure. Venus in Leo is passionate and demands a lot of attention from those they are in relationship with. They are likely to have a glamorous appearance and prefer glitzy apparel. They also often have expensive, luxurious tastes and are generous gift givers. If you have Venus in Leo, you have the kind of energy that turns heads when you walk into a room, and you love it when all eyes are on you.

MARS IN LEO

Mars represents your will, your drive, and your energy. In Leo, this means strong-willed leadership that bursts onto the scene and stays there. This energy is passionate and sustaining, meaning that Mars in Leo will keep going at a faster pace for a longer period of time than anyone around them. They have tons of charisma and self-confidence, and they are exceedingly assertive. If you have this placement, be aware that you can also be extremely bossy to those around you—you are hard to keep up with.

JUPITER IN LEO

Jupiter represents expansion, faith, truth, and freedom but also grandiosity. Jupiter in Leo is flamboyant, generous, and charismatic. These people have the biggest hearts and lots of energy and dynamism, but they can also be rather vain. If you have this placement, keep in mind that you can be decadent and way over-the-top for some people. Overall, though, the fun and heart of Leo combined with the generosity and optimism of Jupiter is a dynamic and expansive energy that inspires all around.

SATURN IN LEO

Saturn represents mastery, determination, and discipline. Saturn in Leo is very strong-willed, determined, and ambitious, but there is a rigidity to this placement that restrains the usual Leo exuberance and fun. It's not an easy placement for a younger individual, but Saturn improves with age, so you will loosen up and allow the dramatic edge out more and more. Saturn is also business oriented, and you may be attracted to the business side of the performance industry.

URANUS IN LEO

Uranus represents individuality, unpredictability, and unconventionality. If you have Uranus in Leo, you likely are very strong-willed, rebellious, dynamic, and a risk-taker. Uranus in Leo is a leader in invention and not afraid to go "where no man has gone before." Be aware that your incredibly ambitious nature can lead you to be rather aggressive as you push through to the top.

NEPTUNE IN LEO

Neptune represents inspiration, illusion, psychic sensitivity, healing, and confusion. Neptune in Leo has charisma and an infectious idealism and zest for life. They are magnetic and creative and can be somewhat of a Svengali, almost hypnotizing those around them. If you have this placement, you may be drawn to work in film or television or using visual media as a form of escapism.

PLUTO IN LEO

Pluto is the soul or the soul's desire. Pluto spends approximately 20 years in each sign, so the mighty dwarf planet's influence is generational, which means that everyone in a generation is influenced by the sign that Pluto is in. The house placement must be blended with the generational concepts to get a clear picture for your own natal cosmic blueprint.

Pluto was in Leo from 1939 to 1957 and returns in 2185. Those born with Pluto in Leo are and will be marked by self-actualization and self-expression. The former is a generation that felt they had a special destiny to fulfill. Steve Jobs, Hillary Clinton, and Bill Gates were all born with Pluto in Leo.

SOUTH NODE IN LEO

If you have the South Node in Leo, you are learning to release the instinctive soul habit of seeking approval from others. You have a tendency to go to extremes so that you get the attention you crave, and this can make you melodramatic and prone to risk-taking.

NORTH NODE IN LEO

If you have the North Node in Leo, you are learning to develop your individuality and self-confidence. You have a tendency to feel as if you don't fit in unless you follow the herd. Your evolutionary purpose is to leave that behind and lead with heart and enthusiasm.

LEO THROUGH THE HOUSES

The house where Leo falls in your natal chart brings deeper insights into those areas of life in which you are dramatic, magnetic, and playful. This is where you are a natural leader. Bring your awareness to how you might also be melodramatic or arrogant in this area.

Shamanic Journey to the Sun, Ruler of Leo

In this exercise you are going to journey to non-ordinary reality, the upper world, in a practice called shamanic journey work. This is similar to a meditation but enables you to actively ask for guidance and answers. Shamanic journey work is an amazing practice for getting support in life. You can take a shamanic journey as often as you would like.

For this journey, search the term "Shamanic Drumming" on YouTube or your preferred video-streaming platform. Pick a track that is 10 to 15 minutes long. (I especially enjoy tracks by Shamanic Experience or Sandra Ingerman.) Experiment with two or three and decide which one feels right for you. It is best to listen using headphones or on high volume. Start the track once you have gotten comfortable.

Either lie on a comfortable blanket or sit comfortably with both feet on the ground. Start the track and close your eyes.

Picture yourself in a starting place. Mine is a meadow, but yours might be a beach, a mountain, a forest, or any other place. Always trust what comes to you.

When you have pictured yourself in that place, look around to see if you have any spirit guides with you (commonly animals or other allies, which might include mythical creatures or even plants and trees). Ask your spirit guide(s) to journey with you. Next, look for a way to the upper world. It might be a ladder, stairs, or a beanstalk, or you may simply fly. Again, trust what comes to you.

Now imagine yourself journeying to the Sun, the ruler of Leo. Take note of everything that happens. Have a conversation with the Sun by asking questions.

How can the Sun help you grow in the area of your chart where the Sun and/or Leo are?

How can the Sun and Leo support you with your personal growth?

The Sun might respond by suggesting how you can learn to shine and have confidence in the area of your chart inhabited by the Sun or Leo or, alternatively, how you can develop your leadership qualities. Remember, this is a conversation where you are seeking to develop your energies in the best way possible for you.

When the conversation is over, thank the Sun and return to your starting place. When you are ready to open your eyes, journal about your experience.

LEO IN THE FIRST HOUSE

If you have Leo in or on the cusp of the first house, you come across as warm, friendly, and open with a sunny appearance. You are magnetic, and people are drawn to your sense of joy and fun. You are the sort of person who lights up a room and gathers everyone around you for attention and affection. People really enjoy being around you.

LEO IN THE SECOND HOUSE

If you have Leo in or on the cusp of the second house, you enjoy using your natural shine and magnetism to attract abundance. You like to live like royalty with a lush garden, fabulous food, and luxurious surroundings, and the more riches you have, the better you feel about yourself. The challenge of Leo here is to find self-worth from within rather than from external riches. You may earn your money through public performance.

LEO IN THE THIRD HOUSE

If you have Leo in or on the cusp of the third house, you enjoy lively company and conversations, and you are likely to be quite dramatically expressive and very entertaining but also rather domineering. You have a compelling and commanding presence and probably have a strong voice, but others can find that somewhat overwhelming at times. Because Leo is a fixed sign, you can be quite fixed in your ideas and need to learn to be more open to other people's ideas and opinions.

LEO IN THE FOURTH HOUSE

If you have Leo in or on the cusp of the fourth house, your home is your palace, and you love those who visit to be wowed by the splendor and glamour. Leo in the fourth house likes to be the center of attention in their home, which can make it difficult for others in their family. Learn to open up your big heart to give as well as receive. Both Leo and Cancer, the sign that naturally rules the fourth house, are extremely sensitive to criticism, so you can be easily hurt.

LEO IN THE FIFTH HOUSE

If you have Leo in or on the cusp of the fifth house, the house ruled by Leo, you are very creative, dramatic, and playful. You take great joy in your hobbies and are likely to enjoy music, singing, and drama. You love being around children and enjoy childlike pastimes. There's such a joyful, loving energy to this placement, but beware that some people can find this energy a little too much to be around for long.

LEO IN THE SIXTH HOUSE

If you have Leo in or on the cusp of the sixth house, you take great pride in your work and you love to receive praise and rewards for all that you do. Without praise and reward, you may feel uninspired and lose interest in doing the work. As this is the house of service, it is helpful to learn to lead with the spirit of service and rely less on the approval of others.

LEO IN THE SEVENTH HOUSE

Leo in or on the cusp of the seventh house indicates that you are attracted to a partner or significant other who is strong and magnetic. You want someone who takes the lead and who takes care of responsibilities, but the issue here is that this can also attract someone who is possessive and controlling. Ideally, you will seek out those who have those strong leadership qualities but who also allow you your intellectual freedom.

LEO IN THE EIGHTH HOUSE

If you have Leo in or on the cusp of the eighth house, you have a tendency to take control of joint financial dealings and not let others have much of a say. On a soul level, you are likely to be prepared to leap into the metaphysical realms and become quite a leader in these fields as you shine your light into the darker realms.

LEO IN THE NINTH HOUSE

If you have Leo in or on the cusp of the ninth house, you have great faith in yourself and your beliefs. You are likely to be a leader in philosophical pursuits or higher education but may be overly focused on status and have a tendency toward intellectual superiority. You love to learn, teach, and travel.

LEO IN THE TENTH HOUSE

Leo in or on the cusp of the tenth house indicates that you desire public recognition and desire to shine in your field. You have great staying power and can accomplish anything you put your mind to. Because Leo wants to shine, be mindful of not blocking the light of others. The best leaders bring out the light in those they lead.

LEO IN THE ELEVENTH HOUSE

If you have Leo in or on the cusp of the eleventh house, you are likely to have a large group of admirers or casual acquaintances because you love to socialize and your magnetism attracts a lot of people to you. As this is also the home of social and/or political causes, you are likely to lead groups in this area but must be mindful of the humanitarian needs of those you lead rather than doing it for your own status.

LEO IN THE TWELFTH HOUSE

Leo is all about leadership and playfulness. Those with Leo in or on the cusp of the twelfth house—the house of the collective unconscious and connection to the muse and mystery—tend to lead behind the scenes and to enjoy the playfulness of their own connection to the collective unconscious. The usually large Leo ego is muted here, but be aware that you can be generous to a fault.

LEO CASE STUDY

Molly has the following placements in her chart:

- Sun in Leo in the second house
- Moon in Virgo in the second house
- Cancer Ascendant

In this example, we are looking only at the Sun, Moon, and Ascendant, but the case study in Appendix A on page 213 integrates other elements in the natal chart.

Molly loves to perform and be on the stage but suffers from terrible stage fright. This is not uncommon with a Cancer Ascendant. Through her work with her natal chart, Molly identifies herself as a natural performer (Sun in the second house) who is very self-critical (Virgo Moon in the second house) and who seems to be very private and shy on first meeting. With a Virgo Moon in the second house and Cancer Ascendant, Molly's fiery second house Sun is able to attend to details, but she is probably her own worst critic. The Cancer Ascendant suggests that she prefers to shine behind the scenes.

Molly's chart helps her understand that she is initially shy (Cancer Ascendant) and hypercritical of herself (Virgo Moon), so she may choose to learn breathing techniques to help her relax and focus on the moment so that she can manage the stage fright.

THE SOUL IN LEO

The personality and behavior of Leo, or any Sun sign, is affected by all the other placements and aspects in the natal chart. This is why it is important to gradually blend the meanings of the planets, signs, houses, aspects, and transits to create an overall picture of the potential in your personal blueprint.

If Leo is your Sun sign, you may have things in common with other Leo Sun signs, but you are uniquely you. For example, a Leo Sun with Libra Ascendant will be really attractive and fun to be around, whereas a Leo Sun with Capricorn Ascendant will be much more reserved than some Leos. Another example is a person with a Leo Sun and Sagittarius Moon, who is fiery and on the move a lot of the time, compared with a person with a Leo Sun and Scorpio Moon, who would likely be more determined and very shrewd.

Leo Strategies to Improve Self-Love Skills

Leo rules the heart, but that sensitive ego of Leo seeks outer approval and love, whereas self-love would enable the Leo soul to both give and receive without that need for approval. These exercises will help you work through your tendency to seek outside approval:

1. Go to YouTube or your favorite video-streaming platform and search for a guided meditation on self-love. You can also download an audio file. Listen to the guided self-love meditation regularly.

2. Treat yourself regularly to something that is for you alone and that brings you joy without any external validation. It could be a long bubble bath, a massage, a good book, or a movie. Leo needs a lot of external praise, and if you use these treats to praise yourself often, the need for praise from others will lessen. Be your own cheerleader and reward yourself.

3. Mirror work is also a useful tool to develop self-love skills. Stand or sit in front of a mirror and look yourself in the eye. Then talk to yourself. Start by telling yourself, "I love you." Then move on to other things that are great about you and heap praise on yourself. Verbally give yourself all the approval you are looking for from others. Do this every day for at least 21 days.

Here are a few things to consider to help you to make the most of your Leo energy in different areas of life. Always consider that your soul chose the Leo energy so that you could be more of a leader and be self-expressive in that area of life. You can choose to maximize the positive energies of Leo.

GENERAL PERSONAL DEVELOPMENT

One issue that causes the most problems for Leo is their tendency to "lord it over others" (be domineering and arrogant), treating people as if they are Leo's royal subjects. A better choice for you would be to become a role model for others, leading by example and inspiring them.

RELATIONSHIPS/RELATING TO OTHERS

Leo's opposite sign is Aquarius, the sign of originality, inventiveness, and personal freedom, so it is good for Leo to work on developing a more detached quality when they relate to others. This isn't to suggest that you should become completely like Aquarius—only that you should infuse some of these qualities in your dealings with others to have more successful relationships.

ACHIEVING GOALS

Leo is a fixed sign and generally has less trouble than most other signs when it comes to completing something they have put their mind to. However, they may be inflexible in their goals, so it would be good to practice being open to shifting gears or trajectory so that you don't become disheartened when things don't go according to plan.

CAREERS

For a full analysis of what type of career you would be suited to, take into account the cusp of the tenth house (the Midheaven), the ruler of that sign, and any planets in the tenth house. For example, a person with a Leo Sun may have Aries on the cusp of the tenth house, and their Sun (ruler of Leo) in the first house. This person would be ideal for leadership roles in many capacities.

Sun and Leo Journaling Exercise

Choose a quiet time and place to look at your natal chart and have your journal handy. Identify the Sun and Leo in your chart. Look at the sign placement of the Sun and the house placement of both the Sun and Leo. You can look at Leo in the houses (see page 93) to get a feel for what the Sun in the houses may also mean.

In your journal, write down keywords and phrases from this book and from your shamanic journey to the Sun. Reflect on how you manifest these energies in your life and how you might choose to develop these energies in a more conscious rather than reactive way. For example, you may have the Sun or Leo in the third house and realize that you are not making full use of your powerful speaking and vocal abilities. With this awareness, you might choose to take drama classes or begin public speaking. Record your reflections in your journal.

Through this journal exercise and your shamanic journey to the Sun, you will begin to really understand the energies in your chart. Through that awareness, you will be able to choose *how* you embody the energies of the Sun and Leo in your life.

virgo the virgin

The first duty of a human being is to assume the right functional relationship to society— more briefly, to find your real job, and do it. —CHARLOTTE PERKINS GILMAN

Dates: August 20–September 20, depending on the year

ELEMENT	MODALITY	RULING PLANET	HOUSE RULED
Earth	Mutable	Mercury	Sixth

Virgo is a mutable Earth sign and is ruled by Mercury. It's the sixth sign in the zodiac and is where we enter adulthood and the world of work.

Virgo is represented by the Virgin. Notice that the glyph for Virgo looks like a coiled *M*; it is often said to represent the intestines, as the sign of Virgo and the sixth house are associated with health and digestive issues. The *M* could also be said to represent Mother, the Madonna, and the biblical Virgin Mary, which give indications of the meanings of this sign.

The Virgin is one of the most complex and misunderstood symbols due to our association with sexual virginity. The etymology of the word *virgin* is complex; one early definition was an "unmarried or chaste woman noted for religious piety and having a position of reverence in the Church." In many Greek translations, it means "one who is whole unto herself." The Greek translation is a powerful one because it suggests someone who is self-sufficient and self-possessed. Since we all have Virgo energy within us, this is where we are self-contained, grounded, and also reverential or service oriented.

One of the best descriptors for the sign of Virgo is "useful." Virgo is practical, attentive to details, and embodies the principle of service. In other words, Virgo loves to be useful. Virgo is usually efficient, organized, and hardworking. It is the sign that is most associated with any skills that require attention to detail and hand skills. For example, someone with the Sun in Virgo in the ninth house might seek to be useful in the areas of religion and/or travel. This person would be drawn to service and ethics in those areas, constantly analyzing how these expansive areas of life can best be of use to the self and others.

When unaware, Virgo energy can possess a servant-like mentality and influence someone to seek perfection, obsess over details, and be overly critical of themselves and others. With awareness, Virgo can choose to release the idea of perfection and take a break from the details.

Now that you have a general feel for Virgo energy, we'll look at *how* the planets show up in Virgo and the houses. With your chart in hand, look for *which* planets you have in Virgo, *how* the planets work in that sign, and *where* in the chart they are—the house. Then you will blend the energies by identifying keywords and phrases from all three that have meaning for you, remembering that you can replace them with any synonyms or phrases with the same meaning of your choosing. With this list, you will create a coherent and meaningful picture to get a deep understanding of how Virgo energy manifests within you. This is where the real awareness and choice comes in. Armed with this knowledge, you can choose how you respond and react to Virgo energy and how you manifest it in the world.

PLANETS IN VIRGO

This section gives you a brief description of each planet in the sign Virgo. I encourage you not to treat these discussions as definitive descriptions but as a springboard for your own interpretation using similar words and themes. You are invited to use these descriptions and the exercises in this chapter to create your own description of how the energy of Virgo and the planets show up within you.

MOON IN VIRGO

The Moon represents your emotional body, and in Virgo, this means you are happiest when you are busy with the simple details of life and when you feel you are being useful to others. People with Virgo Moon are self-effacing and prefer to be in the background organizing and creating routines. Lack of routine and organization is very stressful to those with this placement, and they can become finicky, nervous hypochondriacs if there is a lack of self-awareness. Creating a clean, simple daily life with an attention to healthy routines will bring you contentment.

MERCURY IN VIRGO

Mercury represents communication and thought processes, and Mercury is both the ruler of and said to be exalted in Virgo, so Mercury is at its best here. If you have Mercury in Virgo, you are able to take in a lot of information and skillfully organize it so that it makes sense. You speak clearly and precisely, getting straight to the point, and also have a dry wit that softens the edge of this highly efficient placement. Be aware, however, that you tend to be impatient with people who are less organized and can be highly critical of them.

VENUS IN VIRGO

Venus represents love, relationships, pleasure, creativity, and the value we place on the material things in life and our own pleasure. Venus in Virgo is reserved and discriminating, often seeking perfection in their relationships and in their material surroundings, which leads to hypercriticism of both themselves and others. Venus in Virgo desires all things to be practical and useful, and this applies to their relationships, too. With this placement, you find more meaning in helping others organize their lives than you find in big displays of affection.

MARS IN VIRGO

Mars represents your will, your drive, and your energy. In Virgo, this means you are often driven to do useful acts, to take action that really helps others. Analytical Virgo will quickly assess which actions will be most effective and then do them. This placement can be high-strung and experience a buildup of nervous energy that may result in physical symptoms if a healthy way of expending this energy isn't found. If you have Mars in Virgo, an active, practical daily routine will keep you from feeling frustrated.

JUPITER IN VIRGO

Jupiter represents expansion, faith, truth, and freedom but also grandiosity. Jupiter in Virgo will take on major tasks so that they can make sure they are done well, and their attention to detail and order often brings success. This is generally a highly productive placement. However, Virgo's aversion to risk can also mean they make things harder than they need to be. If you have this placement, be aware that you may get so stuck in the detail that you lose Jupiter's ability to see the bigger picture.

SATURN IN VIRGO

Saturn represents mastery, determination, and discipline. Saturn in Virgo is extremely serious and hardworking. They will be able to achieve a lot in any area that requires dedication and attention to detail but can isolate themselves in their attempt to control everything in their environment. If you have Saturn in Virgo, you tend to live to work. It would be really helpful for you to learn to lighten up a little so that you can step back from work to play occasionally.

URANUS IN VIRGO

Uranus represents individuality, unpredictability, and unconventionality. If you have Uranus in Virgo, you have the ability to meticulously and comprehensively connect a lot of details to create something innovative over time. This placement has an amazing intellect running inside their heads, like a supercomputer running thousands of processes per second. Interested in both the natural world and the technological world, with this placement you are able to use your analytical, inventive, and natural hand skills to create something innovative from what is already present.

NEPTUNE IN VIRGO

Neptune represents inspiration, illusion, psychic sensitivity, healing, and confusion. Neptune in Virgo is concerned with the relationship between mental, spiritual, and physical health. With the tendency of Virgo to overanalyze, this can lead to anxiety and nervousness while Virgo tries to make sense of nebulous Neptune energy. If you have this placement, you will find it helpful to counteract this by being useful to others and the world in general, perhaps in the area of holistic physical health.

PLUTO IN VIRGO

Pluto is the soul or the soul's desire. Pluto spends approximately 20 years in each sign, so the mighty dwarf planet's influence is generational, which means that everyone in a generation is influenced by the sign that Pluto is in. The house placement must be blended with the generational concepts to get a clear picture for your own natal cosmic blueprint.

Pluto was in Virgo from 1956 to 1972 and will return in 2204. Those born with Pluto in Virgo are a generation that is focused on service to the greater good through learning and developing practical ways to resolve the world's problems. Barack Obama, Madonna, Whitney Houston, and Jim Carrey were all born with Pluto in Virgo.

SOUTH NODE IN VIRGO

If you have the South Node in Virgo, you are learning to release the instinctive soul habit of only valuing the self when you are serving others, often to the point of complete self-sacrifice. You are also likely to be overly analytical and critical of yourself and others with almost compulsive perfectionism.

NORTH NODE IN VIRGO

If you have the North Node in Virgo, you are learning to develop your engagement with the outer world and moving toward helping others in some way. You have a tendency to avoid planning and routine and therefore are learning to find the value in those skills.

VIRGO THROUGH THE HOUSES

The house where Virgo falls in your natal chart brings deeper insights into those areas of life in which you are compassionate and bring order. This is where you are naturally drawn to skills that are useful. Bring your awareness to how you might also be overanalytical and a perfectionist.

Shamanic Journey to Mercury, Ruler of Virgo

In this exercise, you are going to journey to non-ordinary reality, the upper world, in a practice called shamanic journey work. This is similar to a meditation but enables you to actively ask for guidance and answers. Shamanic journey work is an amazing practice for getting support in life. You can take a shamanic journey as often as you would like.

For this journey, search the term "Shamanic Drumming" on YouTube or your preferred video-streaming platform. Pick a track that is 10 to 15 minutes long. (I especially enjoy tracks by Shamanic Experience or Sandra Ingerman.) Experiment with two or three and decide which one feels right for you. It is best to listen using headphones or on high volume. Start the track once you have gotten comfortable.

Either lie on a comfortable blanket or sit comfortably with both feet on the ground. Start the track and close your eyes.

Picture yourself in a starting place. Mine is a meadow, but yours might be a beach, a mountain, a forest or any other place. Always trust what comes to you.

When you have pictured yourself in that place, look around to see if you have any spirit guides with you (commonly animals or other allies, which might include mythical creatures or even plants and trees). Ask your spirit guide(s) to journey with you. Next, look for a way to the upper world. It might be a ladder, stairs, or a beanstalk, or you may simply fly. Again, trust what comes to you.

Now imagine yourself journeying to Mercury, the ruler of Virgo. Take note of everything that happens and have a conversation with Mercury by asking questions.

How can Mercury help you grow in the area of your chart where Mercury and/or Virgo reside?

How can Mercury and Virgo support you with your personal growth?

Mercury might respond by suggesting how you can learn to create more order or learn something useful in the area of your chart inhabited by Mercury or Virgo or, alternatively, how you can develop your focus on service. Remember, this is a conversation where you are seeking to develop your energies in the best way possible for you.

When the conversation is over, thank Mercury and return to your starting place. When you are ready to open your eyes, journal about your experience.

VIRGO IN THE FIRST HOUSE

If you have Virgo in or on the cusp the first house, you come across as neat and orderly. These are the people who take detailed notes and make lists so that they can be highly organized and attend to every single detail. Because the first house is how others see you and Virgo needs to get everything right, be aware that you may tend to overwork out of nervousness, seeking to get everything "just so".

VIRGO IN THE SECOND HOUSE

If you have Virgo in or on the cusp of the second house, you enjoy using your organizational abilities to keep track of your finances and to make financial plans. You would make a good financial planner, although your risk aversion can lead to excessive worry. You are able to make money through any work that requires structure and routine.

VIRGO IN THE THIRD HOUSE

If you have Virgo in or on the cusp of the third house, you are always taking in, analyzing, and organizing data and information. You are constantly feeding your mind, and you are excellent at anything requiring logic and reason. The issue can be in the sharing of that information, however. Your perfectionism can keep you from thinking you know enough to share, and, when you do share, you are likely to be attached to others doing things exactly as you think they should be done. Learning to release some of that perfectionism would be helpful.

VIRGO IN THE FOURTH HOUSE

If you have Virgo in or on the cusp of the fourth house, your home and your personal life are likely to be regimented and orderly, and you are unhappy if you are unable to maintain that orderliness. This can be hard on others in your home, however, as your family will feel that you are overly critical. It's important to allow others to be who they are.

VIRGO IN THE FIFTH HOUSE

Virgo in or on the cusp of the fifth house likes structured and planned hobbies and creativity. You probably prefer quieter hobbies that require mental activity. Be aware that overplanning can lead to less joy and fun though. Also, because you have almost impossibly high standards, try to soften your tendency to be overly critical of your children and/or those you are in relationships with.

VIRGO IN THE SIXTH HOUSE

If you have Virgo in or on the cusp of the sixth house, the house ruled by Virgo, your work and daily routines are of paramount importance to you. You work best at anything that uses detail, hand skills, and requires your utmost attention, especially if you are serving others. Be wary of getting so lost in detail and perfectionism that you have trouble finishing projects. You are also likely concerned about staying healthy.

VIRGO IN THE SEVENTH HOUSE

Virgo in or on the cusp of the seventh house indicates that you are attracted to a partner or significant other who helps you get in touch with reality and brings the practical aspects of life into your relationship. This can also represent parts of you that have been repressed due to cultural or familial constraints (known as the disowned or shadow self), and you therefore tend to seek them in others.

VIRGO IN THE EIGHTH HOUSE

If you have Virgo in or on the cusp of the eighth house, you are cautious and detailed when it comes to joint finances and are good at any detail required. However, you tend to worry excessively if things aren't going the way you planned. On a soul level, you are likely to investigate the metaphysical and the deep psyche with the same analytical approach and have an interest in using that to heal. You may be drawn to some forms of psychology.

VIRGO IN THE NINTH HOUSE

If you have Virgo in or on the cusp of the ninth house, you likely study belief systems and cultures in a systematic and detailed way. You are likely to be almost puritanical about how you live out your beliefs and how you expect others to do so. Be aware that you can be critical if you slip from the prescribed track.

VIRGO IN THE TENTH HOUSE

Leo in or on the cusp of the tenth house indicates that you do best in a public role that stimulates your analytical mind and organizational abilities. You are drawn to more conventional roles and not arenas where you are in the spotlight. Any career or mission in life that involves creating structure and is service oriented will be a fit for you.

VIRGO IN THE ELEVENTH HOUSE

If you have Virgo in or on the cusp of the eleventh house, you are likely to have a small group of close friends that you are extremely loyal to. You are the one who will attend to details and organization in a group rather than taking the lead, and you are also the practical voice who can bring dreams into reality.

VIRGO IN THE TWELFTH HOUSE

As Virgo is all about service and organization, if you have Virgo in or on the cusp of the twelfth house, the house of the collective unconscious and connection to the muse and mystery, you have the ability to be a practical mystic, taking complex spiritual ideals and bringing them down to earth. The challenge here is that the selfless energy of the twelfth house can lead to a habit of martyrdom, always giving too much of yourself for the good of others.

VIRGO CASE STUDY

Nick has the following placements in his chart:

- Sun in Virgo in the eleventh house
- Moon in Libra in the twelfth house
- Scorpio Ascendant

In this example, we are looking only at the Sun, Moon, and Ascendant, but the case study in Appendix A on page 213 integrates other elements in the natal chart.

Nick finds that he is often told he is too sensitive and spends a lot of time questioning what's wrong with him. Through his work with his chart, Nick identifies as a group organizer (Sun in the eleventh house) who is very empathic and shy (Cancer Moon in the twelfth house) and who seems to be very private yet magnetic on first meeting (Scorpio Ascendant). With a Cancer Moon in the twelfth house and Scorpio Ascendant, Nick's analytical and perfectionist eleventh house Sun is very much inclined to work in the background and is happiest working in a discreet organizational capacity that helps others.

Nick's chart suggests that he is best working in organizations where he can use his strong organizational abilities (Virgo Sun) to carry out other people's plans (Libra Moon). This would enable him to stay out of self-criticism, since he will be following someone else's rules.

THE SOUL IN VIRGO

The personality and behavior of Virgo, or any Sun sign, is affected by all the other placements and aspects in the natal chart. This is why it is important to gradually blend the meanings of the planets, signs, houses, aspects, and transits to create an overall picture of the potential in your personal blueprint.

If Virgo is your Sun sign, you may have things in common with other Virgo Sun signs, but you are uniquely you. For example, a Virgo Sun with Taurus Ascendant will be much more accepting of others, whereas a Virgo Sun with Gemini Ascendant will be more sociable and able to communicate all that is going on in their head. Another example is a person with a Virgo Sun and Leo Moon who will be more likely to seek the spotlight than a person with Virgo Sun and Cancer Moon, who would be very inclined to introversion.

Virgo Strategies to Release the Inner Critic and Overanalyzer

One of Virgo's biggest issues is self-criticism, which comes from their inner critic. The following strategies will help you calm that inner voice and also help you understand just how well you actually do things.

1. Virgo is a "mental" sign, so journaling is a good activity for personal development. Write out the worst-case scenario of anything running around in your mind and ask questions around it. Is this true? What are the chances of this actually coming to pass? (Virgo loves statistics.) Then write the best-case scenario and use your logical thinking to assess the likelihood of each scenario. This analysis will help your mind figure out that the optimistic view is often the most rational.

2. In your journal or on a piece of paper, record evidence of the times when things worked out well for you. Take note of things you have done that improved your health, mood, and life. Then write to your inner critic, letting it know that it has been wrong, and your ideas and thoughts have been positive influences on your life. Keep compiling this evidence as proof of your amazing mind.

3. Meditation is difficult but crucial for the overly analytical Virgo mind. Silent meditation may not be best for you, so listen to a recording of nature sounds while meditating—or even better, meditate outside to the sound of the birds or the wind in the trees. Thoughts will inevitably come; see them as clouds drifting by or as waves approaching the shore and receding, and gently allow those thoughts to move on by.

Here are a few things to consider to help you to make the most of your Virgo energy in different areas of life. Always consider that your soul chose the Virgo energy so that you could be more of an organizer and create structure in that area of life. You can choose to maximize the positive energies of Virgo.

GENERAL PERSONAL DEVELOPMENT

One issue that causes the most problems for Virgo is their tendency to overthink everything they do. A better choice for Virgo would be to learn that "done" is better than "perfect." To counteract the tendency to try to reach perfection, you can set strict deadlines for yourself and commit to an end point to complete tasks, though it won't be easy at first.

RELATIONSHIPS/RELATING TO OTHERS

Virgo sits opposite to Pisces, the sign of compassion, dreams, and sensitivity, so it is good for Virgo to work on developing those qualities and becoming comfortable with an element of chaos. This isn't to suggest that you should become completely like Pisces—only that you should infuse some of these qualities in your dealings with others to have more successful relationships.

ACHIEVING GOALS

Virgo is a mutable sign and, as such, enjoys change. Their perfectionism will often keep them determined and focused on doing everything right to reach their goal, but it can also keep them so stuck in the detail that they avoid seeing the other possibilities that a slight change in track would open up, allowing them to more quickly achieve their goals. Try to embrace change on your path toward your goal by looking up from the details.

Mercury and Virgo Journaling Exercise

Choose a quiet time and place to look at your natal chart and have your journal handy. Identify Mercury and Virgo in your chart. Look at the sign placement of Mercury and the house placement of both Mercury and Virgo. You can look at Virgo in the houses (see page 107) to get a feel for what Mercury in the houses may also mean.

In your journal, write down keywords and phrases from this book and from your shamanic journey to Mercury. Reflect on how you manifest these energies in your life and how you might choose to develop these energies in a more conscious rather than reactive way. For example, you may have Mercury or Virgo in the eighth house and realize that you are not making full use of the fabulous analytical abilities to explore deep intimacy or navigate shared financial resources. With this awareness, you might choose to begin a shamanic practice or become a financial advisor. Record your reflections in your journal.

Through this journaling exercise and your shamanic journey to Mercury, you will begin to really understand the energies in your chart. Through that awareness, you will be able to choose *how* you embody the energies of Mercury and Virgo in your life.

CAREERS

For a full analysis of what type of career you would be suited to, take into account the cusp of the tenth house (the Midheaven), the ruler of that sign, and any planets in the tenth house. For example, a person with a Virgo Sun may have Cancer on the cusp of the tenth house, and Mercury (ruler of Virgo) in the eleventh house. This person would be suited to a more nurturing role within a group situation, possibly even teaching others in a low-key way.

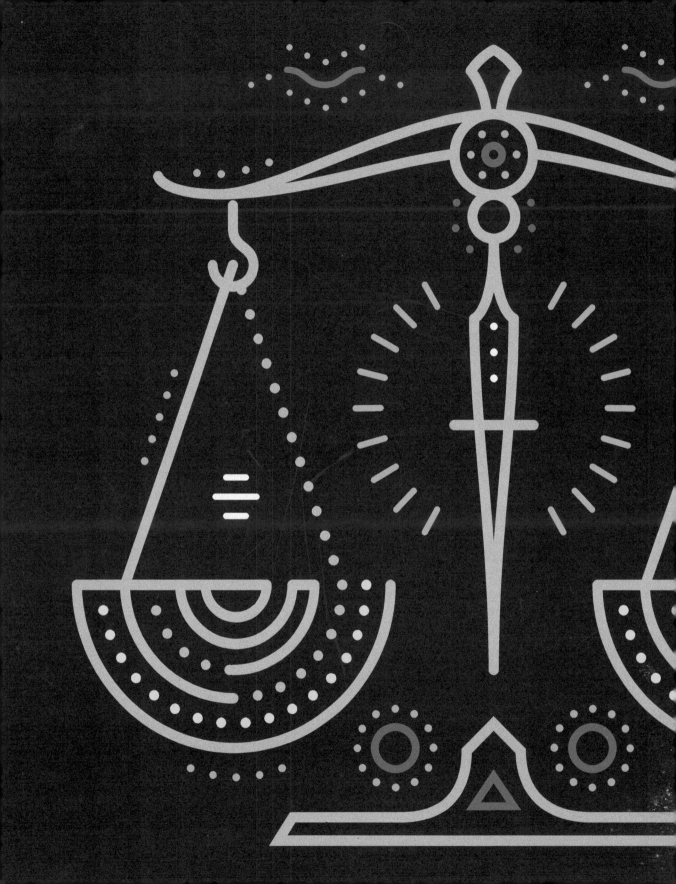

CHAPTER NINE

libra
the scales

The ingredients of both darkness and light are equally present in all of us... The madness of this planet is largely a result of the human being's difficulty in coming to virtuous balance with himself. —ELIZABETH GILBERT, *EAT PRAY LOVE*

Dates: September 20–October 20, depending on the year

ELEMENT	MODALITY	RULING PLANET	HOUSE RULED
Air	Cardinal	Venus	Seventh

Libra is a cardinal Air sign and is ruled by Venus. It's the seventh sign in the zodiac and is where we begin relating to others through relationship.

Libra is represented by the Scales, which indicate balance and justice (scales of justice). The Scales represent impartiality and the weighing of all points of view. Like the Scales, Libra is always seeking the central pivot point, but that is difficult to reach. Libra often leans first one way and then the other. Hence, Libra represents both peace and war, and the temptation is to attempt to create balance by erring on either side of the scale. The evolutionary challenge for Libra is to bring light to situations of disparity without leaning toward one side or the other.

Notice that the glyph for Libra looks like either the sunrise or, in my view, the sunset on the horizon. Since the cusp of the seventh house opposes the Ascendant, or birthline, this indicates that we are moving into a receptive phase where the self is in relationship to the world and must begin to adapt to anything that is "other."

Libra is a receptive Air sign, and Air is associated with the mind. Libra is intelligent, diplomatic, and easygoing. They are usually charming to be around. They are also creative and love beautiful surroundings. The receptivity of Libra can lead to codependence, and they may rely on bouncing their ideas off other people, which also means they can have trouble saying no and seek peace at any price—and that price is usually their own self. For example, the Sun in Libra in the first house would be remarkably congenial and pleasant to be around. This person would be drawn to coming across as considerate and very fair.

In an unaware state, Libra energy can be highly passive-aggressive as they attempt to create balance no matter what they really feel. With awareness, Libra can choose to be true to their own feelings and more assertive in their interactions with others.

Now that you have a general feel for Libra energy, we'll look at *how* the planets show up in Libra and the houses. With your chart in hand, look for *which* planets you have in Libra, *how* the planets work in that sign, and *where* in the chart they are—the house. Then you will blend the energies by identifying keywords and phrases from all three that have meaning for you, remembering that you can replace them with any synonyms or phrases with the same meaning of your choosing. With this list, you will create a coherent and meaningful picture to get a deep understanding of how Libra energy manifests within you. This is where the real awareness and choice comes in. Armed with this knowledge, you can choose how you respond and react to Libra energy and how you manifest it in the world.

PLANETS IN LIBRA

This section gives you a brief description of each planet in the sign Libra. I encourage you not to treat these discussions as definitive descriptions but as a springboard for your own interpretation using similar words and themes. You are invited to use these descriptions and the exercises in this chapter to create your own description of how the energy of Libra and the planets show up within you.

MOON IN LIBRA

The Moon represents your emotional body, and in Libra, the Moon is emotionally more attached to intellectual and artistic pursuits than other pursuits. Libra Moon dislikes anything too deep and disturbing. If you have this placement, you are highly sociable and charming and can feel very emotionally off balance without peace and harmony in your life. You are attracted to things more by fairness and beauty than anything else. You are always polite and considerate and need the same in return. Be aware that at your worst you can be self-indulgent and emotionally dependent.

MERCURY IN LIBRA

Mercury represents communication and thought processes, and in Libra, this represents the natural diplomat and/or debater of the zodiac. With this placement, you can see all sides and points of view, but this can lead to difficulty finding one to settle on. You are fun to be around and like to converse socially, but this will be on the lighter side of life, as Libra rarely likes to delve into the shadows. You may have a musical tone to your speaking voice that others find soothing.

VENUS IN LIBRA

Venus represents love, relationships, pleasure, creativity, and the value we place on the material things in life and our own pleasure. Since Venus is the ruler of Libra, these two are made for each other. This placement is peaceful, cooperative, and full of grace. You strive to create harmonious and balanced relationships with equal respect for each other. Venus in Libra is usually stylish, attractive, and artistic. The only downside of this perfect match is that the focus is so much on exterior light and balanced harmony that the inner self can be neglected in the process.

MARS IN LIBRA

Mars represents your will, your drive, and your energy. Mars likes action and doesn't like waiting around while all options are weighed, so, in Libra, Mars is very frustrated. This frustration can lead to being passive-aggressive. However, there is a good side to this placement. With Mars in Libra, we find the peace warrior or champion of equality. If you have this placement, you can work with others to stir up pubic discussion on behalf of justice and artistry. Remember, you also need others to play with.

JUPITER IN LIBRA

Jupiter represents expansion, faith, truth, and freedom but also grandiosity. Jupiter in Libra is showy romance, hearts, flowers, and a big attraction to fairness and ethics. This placement can also become rather moralistic or dogmatic about what they see as right in relationships and justice. Altruism is the best incarnation of this energy. If you have Jupiter in Libra, use your concern for others to consider their points of review with regard to what they believe is right or just.

SATURN IN LIBRA

Saturn represents mastery, determination, and discipline. Saturn in Libra is just and fair, and would make a good judge. This placement is more self-sufficient than other Libra placements, but it can be a little on the reserved or even cold side emotionally. If you have Saturn in Libra, you work well with others, but be aware that, at times, you may fear not being fair enough and will go to great lengths trying to perfectly balance your relationships and life.

URANUS IN LIBRA

Uranus represents individuality, unpredictability, and unconventionality. If you have Uranus in Libra, you bring the gifts of spontaneity and creativity to your relationships. You are loving, tolerant, and forward thinking. Be sure to give yourself a lot of breathing room so that you never feel prevented from moving forward or making your own choices.

NEPTUNE IN LIBRA

Neptune represents inspiration, illusion, psychic sensitivity, healing, and confusion. Neptune in Libra brings a big dose of empathy and compassion to the usually airy and fairly detached Libra. If you have Libra in Neptune, you are drawn to establishing justice and fairness for the greater good, and because you are also very creative, you may find creative ways to do so.

PLUTO IN LIBRA

Pluto is the soul or the soul's desire. Pluto spends approximately 20 years in each sign, so the mighty dwarf planet's influence is generational, which means that everyone in a generation is influenced by the sign that Pluto is in. The house placement must be blended with the generational concepts to get a clear picture for your own natal cosmic blueprint.

Pluto was in Libra from 1971 to 1984 and will return in 2219. Those born with Pluto in Libra are a generation that is focused on transforming relationships, and there is an almost obsessive need to bring fairness and justice to those arenas. This generation is usually diplomatic in negotiating relationship issues, but occasionally, unfairness will bring volcanic eruptions of anger as Pluto digs in to the underbelly of fairness and justice. Angelina Jolie, Leonardo DiCaprio, Justin Timberlake, and Prince William were all born with Pluto in Libra.

SOUTH NODE IN LIBRA

If you have the South Node in Libra, you are learning to release the instinctive soul habits of niceness and selflessness. You were born codependent and overly attached to fairness and justice. You may need to realize that the scales of justice are difficult to balance exactly. Your evolutionary lesson is to learn self-awareness and independence of thought alongside self-love.

NORTH NODE IN LIBRA

If you have the North Node in Libra, you are learning diplomacy and tact and how to cooperate and collaborate with others through awareness of other people's needs.

Shamanic Journey to Venus, Ruler of Libra

In this exercise, you are going to journey to non-ordinary reality, the upper world, in a practice called shamanic journey work. This is similar to a meditation but enables you to actively ask for guidance and answers. Shamanic journey work is an amazing practice for getting support in life. You can take a shamanic journey as often as you would like.

For this journey, search the term "Shamanic Drumming" on YouTube or your preferred video-streaming platform. Pick a track that is 10 to 15 minutes long. (I especially enjoy tracks by Shamanic Experience or Sandra Ingerman.) Experiment with two or three and decide which one feels right for you. It is best to listen using headphones or on high volume. Start the track once you have gotten comfortable.

Either lie on a comfortable blanket or sit comfortably with both feet on the ground. Start the track and close your eyes.

Picture yourself in a starting place. Mine is a meadow, but yours might be a beach, a mountain, a forest, or any other place. Always trust what comes to you.

When you have pictured yourself in that place, look around to see if you have any spirit guides with you (commonly animals or other allies, which might include mythical creatures or even plants and trees). Ask your spirit guide(s) to journey with you. Next, look for a way to the upper world. It might be a ladder, stairs, or a beanstalk, or you may simply fly. Again, trust what comes to you.

Now imagine yourself journeying to Venus, the ruler of Libra. Take note of everything that happens and have a conversation with Libra by asking questions.

How can Venus help you grow in the area of your chart where Venus and/or Libra reside?

How can Venus support you with your personal growth?

Venus might respond by suggesting how you can learn to put yourself first and help others from a full cup rather than depleting yourself, or, alternatively, how you can develop your self-awareness, as Libra often only sees itself through others. Remember, this is a conversation where you are seeking to develop your energies in the best way possible for you.

When the conversation is over, thank Venus and return to your starting place. When you are ready to open your eyes, journal your experience.

LIBRA THROUGH THE HOUSES

The house where Libra falls in your natal chart brings deeper insights into those areas of life in which you are oriented toward relationships and dependent on others for your self-concept. Bring your awareness to how you might be overly dependent in this area.

LIBRA IN THE FIRST HOUSE

If you have Libra in or on the cusp of the first house, your sense of self is rooted in significant relationships. You see yourself through those relationships and have a hard time being or doing things alone. People see you as graceful and like being around you, but you may feel acutely unbalanced in chaotic environments.

LIBRA IN THE SECOND HOUSE

If you have Libra in or on the cusp of the second house, you will often create wealth through the arts, law, or something connected with beauty, or your money comes through your partner or marriage. You create a harmonious financial life because you feel very off-kilter if your budget isn't balanced. Therefore, even though you like the finer things in life, you go for quality, not quantity, and you don't spend money you don't have.

LIBRA IN THE THIRD HOUSE

If you have Libra in or on the cusp of the third house, you are a graceful communicator who avoids conflict and arguments. Your voice is likely to charm and be quite pleasant, so you would make a good singer or presenter. Although you tend to get thrown off by any sort of conflict, your biggest skill is being able to talk others into compromising without forcing. You'd make a fabulous diplomat.

LIBRA IN THE FOURTH HOUSE

If you have Libra in or on the cusp of the fourth house, you like your home to be a peaceful haven that is usually beautifully and creatively decorated to inspire the harmony you need. The difficulty comes when others create chaos in your home or disrupt your inner peace, throwing you off balance. It would be good for you to learn to accept a small amount of chaos or allow others their chaotic space. You are the mediator in the family and often smooth over the cracks for the sake of keeping the peace.

LIBRA IN THE FIFTH HOUSE

Libra in or on the cusp of the fifth house likes pastimes that involve others rather than doing things alone. You make a very fair parent who tries their best to listen to and understand your children, if you have any. This is a creative placement, but you might not be able to see that in yourself. Hobbies that involve beauty and gentle pursuits suit you better than highly physical sports.

LIBRA IN THE SIXTH HOUSE

If you have Libra in or on the cusp of the sixth house, you work well with others and tend to be the negotiator who comes up with compromises and tries to get everyone to play fair. You enjoy a peaceful and harmonious work environment, but be aware that if you don't have it, your health will suffer.

LIBRA IN THE SEVENTH HOUSE

Libra in or on the cusp of the seventh house indicates that you are attracted to a partner or significant other who makes the relationship about you and how they can support you, which brings balance and harmony to the relationship. Be wary of being all about what you receive from others, and learn the art of compromise so that the other person doesn't feel taken for granted.

LIBRA IN THE EIGHTH HOUSE

If you have Libra in or on the cusp of the eighth house, you are likely to work well with your partner concerning shared financial responsibilities. There can be some difficulty with the Libra tendency toward codependence; you may give your power away to your partner or, conversely, try to control your partner. Compromise and communication are key here.

LIBRA IN THE NINTH HOUSE

If you have Libra in or on the cusp of the ninth house, you enjoy learning about belief systems and other cultures and have an extremely strong sense of fairness and justice philosophically. You may be drawn to ethical studies and teaching about equality and social justice issues.

LIBRA IN THE TENTH HOUSE

Libra in or on the cusp of the tenth house indicates that you function best in a public role where you don't work alone. You are graceful and charming and would do well in fields like the arts or the beauty industry, as well as those that involve diplomacy and mediation. Be aware that you may have difficulty deciding on a career because you tend to spend a long time weighing all the options.

LIBRA IN THE ELEVENTH HOUSE

If you have Libra in or on the cusp of the eleventh house, you are likely to have a large group of friends and try to give them all equal time, which can make you somewhat of a social butterfly. You are the mediator who helps everyone get along. The eleventh house is also the house of long-term goals; you may constantly change what you strive toward, seeking your best fit.

LIBRA IN THE TWELFTH HOUSE

As Libra is all about partnership and collaboration, if you have Libra in or on the cusp of the twelfth house, the house of the collective unconscious and connection to the muse and mystery, you are extremely sensitive to others. You may idealize people you are in relationship with, which can make true partnership difficult. You are highly intuitive and spiritually sensitive, but that can mean you go too far in trying to meet others' spiritual needs and deplete your own. Take care of your own spiritual needs first.

LIBRA CASE STUDY

Alice has the following placements in her chart:

- Sun in Libra in the sixth house
- Moon in Leo in the fifth house
- Taurus Ascendant

In this example, we are looking only at the Sun, Moon, and Ascendant, but the case study in Appendix A on page 213 integrates other elements in the natal chart.

Alice has a well-balanced persona but finds it difficult to follow her gut and is overly reliant on other people's opinions and validation. Through her work with her natal chart, Alice has identified as a natural mediator (Sun in the sixth house) who likes to be playful (Leo Moon in the fifth house) and who seems to be very grounded on first meeting (Taurus Ascendant). With a Leo Moon in the fifth house and Taurus Ascendant, Alice's people-pleasing sixth house Sun is more inclined to stability and has a fabulously playful and heart-led approach to work.

Alice's chart suggests that her she lacks strong Water energy, which usually represents intuition. Choosing to be in or around water physically can help her access the intuition of her gut.

THE SOUL IN LIBRA

The personality and behavior of Libra, or any Sun sign, is affected by all the other placements and aspects in the natal chart. This is why it is important to gradually blend the meanings of the planets, signs, houses, aspects, and transits to create an overall picture of the potential in your personal blueprint.

If Libra is your Sun sign, you may have things in common with other Libra Sun signs, but you are uniquely you. For example, a Libra Sun with Capricorn Ascendant will be much more grounded and disciplined, whereas a Libra Sun with Gemini Ascendant will find it even more difficult to make decisions but will be highly sociable. Another example is a person with a Libra Sun and Aries Moon who will be less prone to codependence than someone with a Libra Sun and Aquarius Moon, who will be constantly in their head and very ungrounded.

Libra Strategies to Release Codependence

Libra has difficulty knowing what their own needs are as they are so focused on others and see themselves as a reflection of others in their life. The following strategies will help you move your focus to your own needs and ground your feelings and thoughts.

1. Spend one hour a week with yourself so that you can determine your personal values, priorities, and beliefs. Put this weekly event on your calendar and stick to it. While you are spending this time with yourself, write any thoughts that come to you in your journal or record yourself on audio.

2. Ground yourself regularly by placing your bare feet on the earth. Whenever you can, remove your shoes and socks and simply feel the earth beneath your feet. Feel the connection to the earth. Do this for a few minutes each day, if possible.

3. Whenever you are having trouble deciding on something, create a list of pros and cons for each of your choices. Then, using this information, choose one option and don't allow yourself to revisit your decision. You will not find this easy at first, but you will achieve far more when you make a choice and follow through on it.

Here are a few things to consider to help you to make the most of your Libra energy in different areas of life. Always consider that your soul chose the Libra energy so that you could be more focused on diplomacy and fairness in that area of life. You can choose to maximize the positive energies of Libra.

GENERAL PERSONAL DEVELOPMENT

One issue that causes the most problems for Libra is their tendency to put everyone else's needs before their own to such a degree that they don't even know what they need. Libra must first develop an understanding of what it means to be loyal to themselves. When you do that, you will realize that the needs of others can only truly be fulfilled when your own needs are met.

RELATIONSHIPS/RELATING TO OTHERS

Libra's opposite sign is Aries—the sign that puts themselves first and is very direct and action oriented. So it is good for Libra to work on developing those qualities and become comfortable with saying "Me first." This isn't to suggest that you should become completely like Aries—only that you should infuse some of these qualities in your dealings with others to have more successful relationships.

ACHIEVING GOALS

Libra is an Air sign that is rarely able to decide what their personal and professional goals are. It's necessary, therefore, for Libra to spend time really getting in touch with their core values and what their goals and dreams are. After you have spent time getting clear, you are likely to need support to achieve your goals since you prefer doing things with others.

CAREERS

For a full analysis of what type of career you would be suited to, take into account the cusp of the tenth house (the Midheaven), the ruler of that sign, and any planets in the tenth house. For example, a person with a Libra Sun may have Capricorn on the cusp of the tenth house and Venus (ruler of Libra) in the seventh house. This person would be suited to more Libra-type roles in the arts or beauty industry, but Capricorn would probably influence them toward the business end of those fields.

Venus and Libra Journaling Exercise

Choose a quiet time and place to look at your natal chart and have your journal handy. Identify Venus and Libra in your chart. Look at the sign placement of Venus and the house placement of both Venus and Libra. You can look at Libra in the houses (see page 123) to get a feel for what Venus in the houses may also mean.

In your journal, write down keywords and phrases from this book and from your shamanic journey to Venus. Reflect on how you manifest these energies in your life and how you might choose to develop these energies in a more conscious rather than reactive way. For example, you may have Venus or Libra in the ninth house and realize that you have not been following your natural inclination to study other belief systems. With this awareness, you might choose to begin a class on world religions or ethics or join a social justice–oriented group. Record your reflections in your journal.

Through this journaling exercise and your shamanic journey to Venus, you will begin to really understand the energies in your chart. Through that awareness, you will be able to choose *how* you embody the energies of Venus and Libra in your life.

CHAPTER TEN

scorpio the scorpion

At the root of every tantrum and power struggle are unmet needs.
—MARSHALL B. ROSENBERG

Dates: October 20–November 20, depending on the year

ELEMENT	MODALITY	RULING PLANET	HOUSE RULED
Water	Fixed	Pluto	Eighth

Scorpio is a fixed Water sign and is ruled by Pluto. It's the eighth sign in the zodiac and is where we merge with all that is "other" to us.

Scorpio is represented by the Scorpion, which brings to mind the stinging tail that Scorpions use when attacked. Scorpio is, however, a deep and complex sign. It is also represented by the snake or serpent, suggesting the transformational shedding of skin and rebirth. The Phoenix is another representation that also symbolizes death and rebirth.

Scorpions hide out in dens, caves, trees, and anywhere else that provides darkness and protection, and this offers a clue to the nature of Scorpio. They prefer to go unnoticed and keep their intense feelings private and internalized to such a degree that they find it exceedingly difficult to express them. Scorpions are not hunters; they hide from predators, but they have sensory hairs on their legs that pick up the vibrations of their prey so they can pounce. In other words, they wait for their food to come to them rather than going out to hunt for it. Those born with this Sun sign have that same deep, vibratory energy that senses everything around them; they are highly intuitive.

As mentioned, Scorpio is a fixed Water sign, and this demonstrates the depths of the inner life of Scorpio. Everything is below the surface yet powerful like the deepest oceans. Scorpio is passionate, intense, obsessive, and powerful. Though they are often described as secretive, I see them as more private about their inner life than secretive. Scorpio is associated with death and rebirth, sex and power, and powerlessness. A Scorpio is not to be underestimated. For example, the Sun in Scorpio in the fifth house would be drawn to transformative hobbies and would be likely to have some very passionate love affairs. They could also be overpowering parents.

In an unaware state, Scorpio energy can be manipulative as they know how to trigger the heartstrings of those close to them to achieve what they desire. With awareness, Scorpio may choose to temper this tendency.

Now that you have a general feel for Scorpio energy, we'll look at *how* the planets show up in Scorpio and the houses. With your chart in hand, look for *which* planets you have in Scorpio, *how* the planets work in that sign, and *where* in the chart they are—the house. Then you will blend the energies by identifying keywords and phrases from all three that have meaning for you, remembering that you can replace them with any synonyms or phrases with the same meaning of your choosing. With this list, you will create a coherent and meaningful picture to get a deep understanding of how Scorpio energy manifests within you. This is where the real awareness and choice comes in. Armed with this knowledge, you can choose how you respond and react to Scorpio energy and how you manifest it in the world.

PLANETS IN SCORPIO

This section gives you a brief description of each planet in the sign Scorpio. I encourage you not to treat these discussions as definitive descriptions but as a springboard for your own interpretation using similar words and themes. You are invited to use these descriptions and the exercises in this chapter to create your own description of how the energy of Scorpio and the planets show up within you.

MOON IN SCORPIO

The Moon represents your emotional body, and in Scorpio, you are loyal and emotionally sensitive. Being so receptive can lead to emotional neediness—a deep urge to merge and almost consume those they love. With this placement, you are highly intuitive and your emotions are so powerful that they can feel quite destructive at times, especially to yourself. Bring awareness to these tendencies so that you can defuse them before they get the better of you.

MERCURY IN SCORPIO

Mercury represents communication and thought processes, and in Scorpio, the mind pierces to the deepest truths. Their passionate nature comes through with intensity when they communicate, and they are always investigating and exploring the motivations of those around them. This is not a placement that enjoys small talk, so talk about the deeper things that are on your mind.

VENUS IN SCORPIO

Venus represents love, relationships, pleasure, creativity, and the value we place on the material things in life and our own pleasure. Venus in Scorpio is somewhat of a femme fatale, attracting people with your charm and mystery. You love intensely, which applies to your relationships, art, money, and beauty. Be aware of a tendency to become possessive in your relationships, but do honor your intense passions.

MARS IN SCORPIO

Mars represents your will, your drive, and your energy. In Scorpio, Mars is very comfortable because it is the traditional ruler of the sign. (Pluto is the modern ruler of this sign.) Mars in Scorpio has immense willpower and drive. Be aware, though, that some can find this immensity overwhelming. If you have Mars in Scorpio, you have intense magnetism and are highly physical and sexual, but you are also emotionally complex.

JUPITER IN SCORPIO

Jupiter represents expansion, faith, truth, and freedom but also grandiosity. Jupiter in Scorpio has larger-than-life emotions, but this placement also has the ability to keep their powerful emotions hidden. They make their own luck and are usually very fortunate in business. If you have Jupiter in Scorpio, you have great confidence and will, but there is a more jovial feel to these qualities than would be found in other placements.

SATURN IN SCORPIO

Saturn represents mastery, determination, and discipline. Saturn in Scorpio is demanding of the self and others. With this placement, you are very driven to succeed, but you also have deep fears of failure and not being enough. These fears can lead to being even more hard on yourself and others. Learning to take a much-needed break every now and again to just be would be helpful.

URANUS IN SCORPIO

Uranus represents individuality, unpredictability, and unconventionality. If you have Uranus in Scorpio, you are strong willed and innovative. In fact, you are somewhat of a force to be reckoned with. The rebelliousness of Uranus gives you the ability to think well outside the box and come up with endless new ideas.

NEPTUNE IN SCORPIO

Neptune represents inspiration, illusion, psychic sensitivity, healing, and confusion. Neptune in Scorpio has a remarkably deep connection to the realms of mystery and the deepest psyche, and they find pleasure in things that many fear. They are often deeply psychic and have addictive tendencies. If you have this placement, bringing awareness to these tendencies can help you harness your abilities and be wary of addictive substances and behaviors.

PLUTO IN SCORPIO

Pluto is the soul or the soul's desire. Pluto spends approximately 20 years in each sign, so the mighty dwarf planet's influence is generational, which means that everyone in a generation is influenced by the sign that Pluto is in. The house placement must be blended with the generational concepts to get a clear picture for your own natal cosmic blueprint.

Pluto was in Scorpio from 1983 to 1995 and will return in 2230. Those born with Pluto in Scorpio are a generation that is focused on delving into areas like genetic engineering and other forms of deep research. If they don't do it themselves, they have an interest in it. Taylor Swift, Prince Harry, and Mark Zuckerberg were all born with Pluto in Scorpio.

SOUTH NODE IN SCORPIO

If you have the South Node in Scorpio, you are learning to release the instinctive soul habits of inappropriate intensity, being overly preoccupied with other people's psychological motivations, and generally being too focused on others. Your evolutionary lesson here is to learn a true sense of self-worth and knowing your own core values.

NORTH NODE IN SCORPIO

If you have the North Node in Scorpio, you are learning the value of deep emotional connections and releasing attachment to material belongings.

Shamanic Journey to Pluto, Ruler of Scorpio

In this exercise you are going to journey to non-ordinary reality, the upper world, in a practice called shamanic journey work. This is similar to a meditation but enables you to actively ask for guidance and answers. Shamanic journey work is an amazing practice for getting support in life. You can take a shamanic journey as often as you would like.

For this journey, search the term "Shamanic Drumming" on YouTube or your preferred video-streaming platform. Pick a track that is 10 to 15 minutes long. (I especially enjoy tracks by Shamanic Experience or Sandra Ingerman.) Experiment with two or three and decide which one feels right for you. It is best to listen using headphones or on high volume. Start the track once you have gotten comfortable.

Either lie on a comfortable blanket or sit comfortably with both feet on the ground. Start the track and close your eyes.

Picture yourself in a starting place. Mine is a meadow, but yours might be a beach, a mountain, a forest, or any other place. Always trust what comes to you.

When you have pictured yourself in that place, look around to see if you have any spirit guides with you (commonly animals or other allies, which might include mythical creatures or even plants and trees). Ask your spirit guide(s) to journey with you. Next, look for a way to the upper world. It might be a ladder, stairs, or a beanstalk, or you may simply fly. Again, trust what comes to you.

Now imagine yourself journeying to Pluto, the ruler of Scorpio. Take note of everything that happens and have a conversation with Pluto by asking questions.

How can Pluto help you grow in the area of your chart where Pluto and/or Scorpio reside?

How can Pluto support you with your personal growth?

Pluto might respond by suggesting how you can learn to transform your obsessions into actually creating something, or, alternatively, how you can develop patience. Remember, this is a conversation where you are seeking to develop your energies in the best way possible for you.

When the conversation is over, thank Pluto and return to your starting place. When you are ready to open your eyes, journal about your experience.

SCORPIO THROUGH THE HOUSES

The house where Scorpio falls in your natal chart brings deeper insights into those areas of life in which you are intense and investigative. This is where you are naturally drawn to delve deeply into this area of life. Bring your awareness to how you might also be overly obsessive and attached to other people's business.

SCORPIO IN THE FIRST HOUSE

If you have Scorpio in or on the cusp the first house, you have a magnetism and presence that draws people in. You are intensely private about your inner life and deep feelings, which adds to the attraction others feel toward you. Some can find this trait overpowering and intimidating even though you don't necessarily intend it to be so. You simply have this innate power and control that others don't have.

SCORPIO IN THE SECOND HOUSE

If you have Scorpio in or on the cusp of the second house, you have the ability to create a lot of wealth, especially through Scorpio-type fields of transformation, which can apply to personal, financial, or scientific transformation. You will achieve a lot if you get clear about your own core values rather than focusing on other people's business.

SCORPIO IN THE THIRD HOUSE

If you have Scorpio in or on the cusp of the third house, you have strong and often rigid beliefs and opinions. The third house rules perception, and your Scorpio intensity will investigate something until you get to its core because you tend to become obsessed with your research. Your communication style is intense and powerful; be aware that it can be more than a little overwhelming for some.

SCORPIO IN THE FOURTH HOUSE

If you have Scorpio in or on the cusp of the fourth house, this is where you can experience true intimacy once you allow others into your home or inner life. You are loyal to and protective of your family, though your tendency to dominate can mean that you try to make others carry out your desires. Home and family is one place that Scorpio may be able to let their guard down.

SCORPIO IN THE FIFTH HOUSE

Scorpio in or on the cusp of the fifth house likes pastimes that feed their obsessive, research-loving nature so that they can really get to the core of their interests. Any hobby involving research will be of interest to you. Be aware that you are likely to be somewhat overprotective and a little controlling of your children, if you have any. The same can be said of your love affairs.

SCORPIO IN THE SIXTH HOUSE

If you have Scorpio in or on the cusp of the sixth house, you can get rather obsessed with work and routines, which can be exhausting for others who can't keep up with your intensity. You may be drawn to work in the fields of finance, science, or research, where you can work alone.

SCORPIO IN THE SEVENTH HOUSE

Scorpio in or on the cusp of the seventh house indicates that you are attracted to a partner or significant other who is not easily overpowered by your intensity, yet doesn't control you either. You are really looking for deeply bonded relationships and will have to work on treating them as an equal, but your loyalty means that you are generally prepared to do that work.

SCORPIO IN THE EIGHTH HOUSE

If you have Scorpio in or on the cusp of the eighth house, this is double the intensity as Scorpio is the natural ruler of this house. This placement dives deeply into all matters of the eighth house, such as the deep psyche and joint finances. Be aware that there can be power struggles and manipulation in close relationships with this placement. You are likely to be psychic and have a strong connection with the unseen.

SCORPIO IN THE NINTH HOUSE

If you have Scorpio in or on the cusp of the ninth house, you are emotionally invested in belief systems and their power structures. You are more interested in the darker and taboo realms and how they lead to the merging of the self with the unseen.

SCORPIO IN THE TENTH HOUSE

Scorpio in or on the cusp of the tenth house indicates that you are dedicated to your public mission in life. You are seen as focused and powerful. Be aware that your deep emotions can sometimes get in the way of success, so find a way to channel them. You are drawn to help others transform in areas like therapy or finances.

SCORPIO IN THE ELEVENTH HOUSE

If you have Scorpio in or on the cusp of the eleventh house, you choose friends carefully and you are extremely loyal. You are attracted to powerful people and those who share the same strength of will and love of deep topics. You are equally loyal to your goals and are driven to make them reality.

SCORPIO IN THE TWELFTH HOUSE

As Scorpio is all about the deeper realms of the psyche, if you have Scorpio in or on the cusp of the twelfth house, the house of the collective unconscious and connection to the muse and mystery, you are connected to the unconscious to the point of almost being able to merge with the spiritual world. You are very intuitive and psychic but also extremely introverted and private.

SCORPIO CASE STUDY

Richard has the following placements in his chart:

- Sun in Scorpio in the second house
- Moon in Sagittarius in the third house
- Libra Ascendant

In this example, we are looking only at the Sun, Moon, and Ascendant, but the case study in Appendix A on page 213 integrates other elements in the natal chart.

Richard has an issue with being seen as provocative, bossy (Libra Ascendant), and dogmatic (Sagittarius Moon in the third house) at times and wishes to find out why and how to be more approachable. Through his work with his natal chart, Richard identifies as a natural researcher, especially with other people's money (Sun in the second house), who is both a student and teacher (Sagittarius Moon in the third house), and who comes across as a peacemaker (Libra Ascendant). With a Sagittarius Moon in the third house and Libra Ascendant, his intense second house Sun is more inclined to open communication than some other Scorpios.

Richard's chart suggests that he should learn how to pause before speaking dogmatically by counting to three and asking himself, "Is this true for everyone?" This will enable him to listen to others and be more open to new information. With regard to the Libra Ascendant tendency to be provocative, Richard's understanding of his natal chart enables him to become aware of when he is doing this rather than seeking true balance.

THE SOUL IN SCORPIO

The personality and behavior of Scorpio, or any Sun sign, is affected by all the other placements and aspects in the natal chart. This is why it is important to gradually blend the meanings of the planets, signs, houses, aspects, and transits to create an overall picture of the potential in your personal blueprint.

If Scorpio is your Sun sign, you may have things in common with other Scorpio Sun signs, but you are uniquely you. For example, a Scorpio Sun with Sagittarius Ascendant will be much more outgoing and loosened up, whereas a Scorpio Sun with Cancer Ascendant will be doubly private and introverted. Another example is a person with a Scorpio Sun and Taurus Moon who will be more embodied and more able to interact with the material world than someone

Scorpio Strategies to Release Trapped Emotions

Scorpio has difficulty expressing their emotions, as their feelings are often so deep and shadowy that words are hard to find. The following strategies will help you connect with your emotions and learn to express them.

1. To help release your swirling inner feelings, write three pages in longhand of stream-of-consciousness writing on a daily basis. This is a release-of-feelings exercise, so it is not meant to make sense or to be read by anyone else. If you are concerned that someone else might see it—as a Scorpio, this is a good possibility—buy a journal with a lock and/or keep it somewhere safe.

2. Sit comfortably with your feet on the ground and eyes closed. Visualize a root growing from the base of your spine, gradually extending down into the earth and spreading out until you connect with the center of the earth. Feel yourself pulling the earth energy up through the roots and moving the energy up through your body until it fills every part of you and then extends up through the top of your head and connects with your spirit. Keep running the energy through your body until you feel connected with the material world, earth, and spirit. This will help you move the emotional energy that often stays trapped in your body.

3. As soon as you feel yourself exhibiting a flash of anger, take that as a cue to pause. During this pause, take a breath and, if possible, you may want to remove yourself from the situation. Anger can be a transformative energy if it is directed in a healthy way, but Scorpio anger is reactive and painful, which often hurts both the giver and receiver. The pause can help reduce the intensity of the anger.

with a Scorpio Sun and Pisces Moon, who will be extremely intuitive and/or psychic but very ungrounded.

Here are a few things to consider to help you make the most of your Scorpio energy in different areas of life. Always consider that your soul chose the Scorpio energy so that you could be more powerful and deeply interactive in that area of life. You can choose to maximize the positive energies of Scorpio.

GENERAL PERSONAL DEVELOPMENT

One issue that causes the most problems for Scorpio is their obsessive nature. This tendency can be harnessed, however. Scorpio can find fulfillment by learning to channel an obsession into the creation of something meaningful. When you channel this energy into something constructive, you will see the benefits.

RELATIONSHIPS/RELATING TO OTHERS

Opposite from Scorpio is Taurus, the sign of the physical body and nature, so it is good for Scorpio to work on embodiment and grounding in nature so they are not so tightly wound. This isn't to suggest that you should become completely like Taurus—only that you should infuse some of these qualities in your dealings with others to have more successful relationships.

ACHIEVING GOALS

Scorpio is a fixed Water sign that is generally quite good at sticking to and achieving their goals—that is, if they can move past the constant and obsessive need to go deeper and instead step back when their goals are reached. When you have achieved your goal, take a breath and look at what you have accomplished.

CAREERS

For a full analysis of what type of career you would be suited to, take into account the cusp of the tenth house (the Midheaven), the ruler of that sign, and any planets in the tenth house. For example, a person with a Scorpio Sun may have Gemini on the cusp of the tenth house and their Mercury (ruler of Gemini) in the ninth house. This person might be suited to teaching or writing (Gemini in the tenth house) about philosophy or different cultures (Mercury in the ninth house) in great depth (Scorpio Sun).

Pluto and Scorpio Journaling Exercise

Choose a quiet time and place to look at your natal chart and have your journal handy. Identify Pluto and Scorpio in your chart. Look at the sign placement of Pluto and the house placement of both Pluto and Scorpio. You can look at Scorpio in the houses (see page 137) to get a feel for what Pluto in the houses may also mean.

In your journal, write down keywords and phrases from this book and from your shamanic journey to Pluto. Reflect on how you manifest these energies in your life and how you might choose to develop these energies in a more conscious rather than reactive way. For example, you may have Pluto or Scorpio in the tenth house and realize that you have not been following your natural inclination to work in the field of transformation. With this awareness, you might choose to take classes on counseling or maybe even a course on shamanic studies. Record your reflections in your journal.

Through this journaling exercise and your shamanic journey to Pluto, you will begin to really understand the energies in your chart. Through that awareness, you will be able to choose *how* you embody the energies of Pluto and Scorpio in your life.

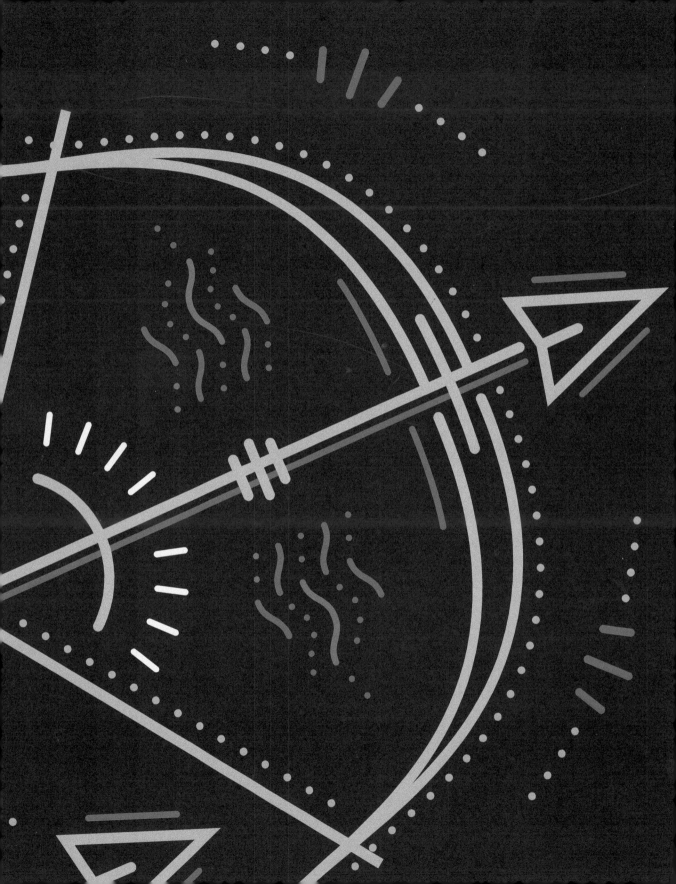

sagittarius the archer

The truth will set you free, but first it will piss you off.
—JOE KLAAS, *TWELVE STEPS TO HAPPINESS*

Dates: November 20–December 20, depending on the year

ELEMENT	MODALITY	RULING PLANET	HOUSE RULED
Fire	Mutable	Jupiter	Ninth

Sagittarius is a mutable Fire sign and is ruled by Jupiter. It's the ninth sign in the zodiac and is where we merge with higher beliefs and perspectives.

Sagittarius is represented by the Archer—the half-man (upper body) and half-horse (lower body) Centaur who is aiming his arrows up to the heavens and toward the future. The Archer suggests that Sagittarius is always seeking truth, freedom, knowledge, and new experiences. The mythical stories of Centaurs are many and the origins are unclear, but generally Centaurs are seen as having traits of both the higher mind (stargazing, astronomy, teaching, and healing) as well as wild and often barbaric tendencies. This is also true of Sagittarius, as they can be the wisest and most excessive of signs.

Sagittarius is an optimistic and enthusiastic sign that is always moving like the flames of a wild fire, dancing and moving on to new ground quickly. They live life as an adventure or vision quest and do not enjoy routine or being constrained in any way. They are idealists and, as such, are often blinded by faith in those ideals until shown that they are not ideal, and then they move on to another.

The adverb *overly* can be used to describe Sagittarius in many ways. Overly idealistic, overly enthusiastic, and overly truthful (blunt). Their immense sense of humor tends to help them get away with it because they are very good-natured at heart. This fast-moving, faith-based idealism can lead them into some intensely risky situations though, and that can be where their lack of judgment and prudence gets them into trouble. For example, the Sun in Sagittarius in the tenth house may have several career changes or even be working on more than one mission in life at the same time because they do not enjoy being pinned down.

In an unaware state, Sagittarius tends toward dogmatism and righteousness, which is ironic for one who is always seeking. Whichever "truth" they have landed on in the moment will be defended vigorously. With awareness, Sagittarius can choose to seek deeper truth and be less defensive.

Now that you have a general feel for Sagittarius energy, we'll look at *how* the planets show up in Sagittarius and the houses. With your chart in hand, look for *which* planets you have in Sagittarius, *how* the planets work in that sign, and *where* in the chart they are—the house. Then you will blend the energies by identifying keywords and phrases from all three that have meaning for you, remembering that you can replace them with any synonyms or phrases with the same meaning of your choosing. With this list, you will create a coherent and meaningful picture to get a deep understanding of how Sagittarius energy manifests within you. This is where the real awareness and choice comes in. Armed with this knowledge, you can choose how you respond and react to Sagittarius energy and how you manifest it in the world.

PLANETS IN SAGITTARIUS

This section gives you a brief description of each planet in the sign Sagittarius. I encourage you not to treat these discussions as definitive descriptions but as a springboard for your own interpretation using similar words and themes. You are invited to use these descriptions and the exercises in this chapter to give you a description of how the energy of Sagittarius and the planets show up within you.

MOON IN SAGITTARIUS

The Moon represents your emotional body, and in Sagittarius, we see the happiest placement in the zodiac. Those with this placement are enthusiastic, inquisitive, and adventurous as long as nothing restricts them. Emotional wonderers and wanderers of the zodiac, Sagittarius Moons are always seeking new horizons in their search for higher truths and new experiences. If you have this placement, you have great candor and often blurt out exactly what you are feeling at any given moment.

MERCURY IN SAGITTARIUS

Mercury represents communication and thought processes, and in Sagittarius, there is in an endless pursuit of knowledge and expansion of the mind. They are big-picture thinkers and teachers, which means they can miss details at times or actually even dismiss details. They can be dogmatic when sharing their thoughts. If you have Mercury in Sagittarius, being aware of these tendencies can help you temper them and share your ideas and lessons more effectively with others.

VENUS IN SAGITTARIUS

Venus represents love, relationships, pleasure, creativity, and the value we place on the material things in life and our own pleasure. Venus in Sagittarius is fun to be around and enthusiastic in love as long as their partners and friends don't restrict their personal freedom. They need a light touch and an intellectual component to their relationships. If you have Venus in Sagittarius, you also exhibit this light touch with money, which means that you are not always the best at managing your finances, so try to be more mindful.

MARS IN SAGITTARIUS

Mars represents your will, your drive, and your energy. Sagittarius in Mars is direct, fun-loving, and likes to get their way and bring others along with them. They dislike it when others don't go their way or poke holes in their visions, and they will often take it personally. With this placement, you have a lot of energy and drive to experience everything you can, which can occasionally turn to risk-taking.

JUPITER IN SAGITTARIUS

Jupiter represents expansion, faith, truth, and freedom but also grandiosity. Jupiter in the sign it rules, Sagittarius, is the biggest seeker of all things Sagittarius and could be said to be the luckiest placement in the zodiac. With Jupiter in Sagittarius, you are warm, outgoing, and explore *everything*. Because of the expansive knowledge and nature of this placement, the only real downside is that some people may see you as a know-it-all.

SATURN IN SAGITTARIUS

Saturn represents mastery, determination, and discipline. Saturn in Sagittarius is serious about study and travel and believes that hard work is needed to achieve mastery in their chosen fields. They also have a fear of never being quite good enough, which makes them work even harder to prove themselves. If you have this placement, know that you can move beyond this fear and become a real authority in any chosen topic.

URANUS IN SAGITTARIUS

Uranus represents individuality, unpredictability, and unconventionality. If you have Uranus in Sagittarius, you are likely to have an unconventional and even eccentric nature. You are a true visionary who may have premonitions and an inventive imagination. You will go your own way and be unlikely to follow traditional fields of study unless you are the one reimagining that field.

NEPTUNE IN SAGITTARIUS

Neptune represents inspiration, illusion, psychic sensitivity, healing, and confusion. Neptune in Sagittarius is likely to be highly intuitive and may have strong psychic abilities. All topics related to faith and belief are of interest, and they are acutely attuned to the collective unconscious. As this is a very idealistic placement, you may have a tendency to fanaticism or being taken in by a guru-type figure. Be on the lookout for this tendency and take a close look at any teacher you may consider following.

PLUTO IN SAGITTARIUS

Pluto is the soul or the soul's desire. Pluto spends approximately 20 years in each sign, so the mighty dwarf planet's influence is generational, which means that everyone in a generation is influenced by the sign that Pluto is in. The house placement must be blended with the generational concepts to get a clear picture for your own natal cosmic blueprint.

Pluto was in Sagittarius from 1995 to 2008 and will return in 2243. Those born with Pluto in Sagittarius are a generation that is tolerant and transforms how we view others and is interested in exploring the idea of transforming higher education and travel. They envision a future that is quite different from previous generations. Mozart, Marie Antoinette, William Blake, and Malala Yousafzai were all born with Pluto in Sagittarius.

SOUTH NODE IN SAGITTARIUS

If you have the South Node in Sagittarius, you are learning to release the instinctive soul habit of needing to be seen as right about everything. To you, your truth is the truth, and you find it difficult to slow down and listen to what others are saying.

NORTH NODE IN SAGITTARIUS

If you have the North Node in Sagittarius, you are learning the value of letting go of an endless search for information to prove what is true and stepping into your intuitive knowing and speaking from a higher consciousness.

SAGITTARIUS THROUGH THE HOUSES

The house where Sagittarius falls in your natal chart brings deeper insights into those areas of life in which you are optimistic and enthusiastic. This is where you are naturally drawn to look for meaning and truth.

Shamanic Journey to Jupiter, Ruler of Sagittarius

In this exercise you are going to journey to non-ordinary reality, the upper world, in a practice called shamanic journey work. This is similar to a meditation but enables you to actively ask for guidance and answers. Shamanic journey work is an amazing practice for getting support in life. You can take a shamanic journey as often as you would like.

For this journey, search the term "Shamanic Drumming" on YouTube or your preferred video-streaming platform. Pick a track that is 10 to 15 minutes long. (I especially enjoy tracks by Shamanic Experience or Sandra Ingerman.) Experiment with two or three and decide which one feels right for you. It is best to listen using headphones or on high volume. Start the track once you have gotten comfortable.

Either lie on a comfortable blanket or sit comfortably with both feet on the ground. Start the track and close your eyes.

Picture yourself in a starting place. Mine is a meadow, but yours might be a beach, a mountain, a forest, or any other place. Always trust what comes to you.

When you have pictured yourself in that place, look around to see if you have any spirit guides with you (commonly animals or other allies, which might include mythical creatures or even plants and trees). Ask your spirit guide(s) to journey with you. Next, look for a way to the upper world. It might be a ladder, stairs, or a beanstalk, or you may simply fly. Again, trust what comes to you.

Now imagine yourself journeying to Jupiter, the ruler of Sagittarius. Take note of everything that happens and have a conversation with Jupiter by asking questions.

How can Jupiter help you grow in the area of your chart where Jupiter and/or Sagittarius reside?

How can Jupiter support you with your personal growth?

Jupiter might respond by suggesting how you can learn to be less dogmatic and develop your listening skills. Remember, this is a conversation where you are seeking to develop your energies in the best way possible for you.

When the conversation is over, thank Jupiter and return to your starting place. When you are ready to open your eyes, journal your experience.

SAGITTARIUS IN THE FIRST HOUSE

If you have Sagittarius in or on the cusp of the first house, people see you as optimistic, fun-loving, and generous. You are always exploring so that you can have as much experience as possible. Your optimism helps others see the world in a more positive light, and people trust your honesty.

SAGITTARIUS IN THE SECOND HOUSE

If you have Sagittarius in or on the cusp of the second house, your self-esteem is more attached to the freedom to explore the world through experience rather than through the accumulation of money. You do, however, have the ability to think long term about your finances so you can plan ahead, but then you are happy to share generously. Travel, teaching, and working with other cultures are all fields where you can make money, but more importantly, these fields give your life meaning.

SAGITTARIUS IN THE THIRD HOUSE

If you have Sagittarius in or on the cusp of the third house, you are always expanding your mind and are the perpetual student, continually studying or taking classes. You need constant mental challenge, but you can get stuck in the learning without applying what you have learned. You are also an enthusiastic and honest communicator who says what you are thinking.

SAGITTARIUS IN THE FOURTH HOUSE

If you have Sagittarius in or on the cusp of the fourth house, you need a spacious home with large windows that has the feeling of bringing the outdoors inside with lots of natural light. Your family is important to you, and you strive to give them the same sense of freedom you need.

SAGITTARIUS IN THE FIFTH HOUSE

If you have Sagittarius in or on the cusp of the fifth house, you like pastimes that are adventurous and give you an experience with a learning element. You like to be free to do things your own way, so structured or sedentary hobbies are not a fit here. Creatively, you have big ideas and enjoy an element of risk. You are a lot of fun, but you may have high expectations of any children you have.

SAGITTARIUS IN THE SIXTH HOUSE

If you have Sagittarius in or on the cusp of the sixth house, you can bring your fabulous teaching ability to serve others, and you are able to bring lightness and fun into your work. While the sixth house energy will bring more organization and structure to the Sagittarius energy, you are still more suited to a daily structure that allows movement and freedom.

SAGITTARIUS IN THE SEVENTH HOUSE

Sagittarius in or on the cusp of the seventh house indicates that you are attracted to a partner or significant other who gives you freedom and won't hold you back from being and doing what you wish. You require someone who can meet you at an intellectual level, and you will move on if your relationships feel clingy or boring.

SAGITTARIUS IN THE EIGHTH HOUSE

If you have Sagittarius in or on the cusp of the eighth house, you love to delve deeply into the human psyche to seek experience and knowledge. You are unafraid to explore where others are afraid to go, exploring people's passions, deeper motivations, and their sexual lives. You are also likely to receive wealth through inheritances or the work of others.

SAGITTARIUS IN THE NINTH HOUSE

If you have Sagittarius in or on the cusp of the ninth house, the house that Sagittarius rules, you have an even greater passion for seeking out experiences and opportunities to learn about spiritual and philosophical beliefs and cultures. You are constantly traveling and on the move, either in your mind or physically. A natural teacher and mentor, you likely teach in some way.

SAGITTARIUS IN THE TENTH HOUSE

Sagittarius in or on the cusp of the tenth house indicates that you have a lovely optimistic and positive attitude about your mission in life. You may have different public roles throughout your life and even have more than one role at a time as you love variety. These roles may involve travel, writing, teaching, and/or working with foreign cultures. You thoroughly enjoy your public work.

SAGITTARIUS IN THE ELEVENTH HOUSE

If you have Sagittarius in or on the cusp of the eleventh house, you are likely to have a large group of friends from all backgrounds and cultures, and you will seek out those you can have philosophical debates with. You may take your natural teaching ability out into the world with a big message, either physically or through the Internet (which is ideal for Sagittarius since it reaches far and wide).

SAGITTARIUS IN THE TWELFTH HOUSE

If you have Sagittarius in or on the cusp of the twelfth house, the house of the collective unconscious and connection to the muse and mystery, you are able to bring some understanding to the nebulous energies of this house and teach difficult concepts. Be wary of overintellectualizing these traits, though; you must allow yourself the *feeling* of experiencing creativity and transcendent states.

SAGITTARIUS CASE STUDY

Jen has the following placements in her chart:

- Sun in Sagittarius in the twelfth house
- Moon in Gemini in the sixth house
- Sagittarius Ascendant

In this example, we are looking only at the Sun, Moon, and Ascendant, but the case study in Appendix A on page 213 integrates other elements in the natal chart.

Jen often finds that she upsets others by being very blunt and quick to speak, and some find her dogmatic. Through her work with her natal chart, Jen identifies as a teacher of creativity or mystical principles (Sun in the twelfth house) who is also learning how to better serve others and organize their teachings (Gemini Moon in the sixth house) and who comes across as jolly, optimistic, and a lot of fun (Sagittarius Ascendant). With a Gemini Moon in the sixth house and Sagittarius Ascendant, her introverted and intuitive twelfth house Sun is more outgoing than others.

Jen's chart suggests that she use her newfound awareness to understand that this is how she works and not everyone works the same way. She might choose to learn simple techniques such as counting to three before speaking reactively, sending emails, or making social media posts. This will give her time to check if what she is about to say is too blunt or not thoughtful enough.

THE SOUL IN SAGITTARIUS

The personality and behavior of Sagittarius, or any Sun sign, is affected by all the other placements and aspects in the natal chart. This is why it is important to gradually blend the meanings of the planets, signs, houses, aspects, and transits to create an overall picture of the potential in your personal blueprint.

If Sagittarius is your Sun sign, you may have things in common with other Sagittarius Sun signs, but you are uniquely you. For example, a Sagittarius Sun with Cancer Ascendant will be shy on first meeting and until you get to know them, whereas a Sagittarius Sun with Gemini Ascendant will be doubly talkative and tactless but a voracious student. Another example is a person with a Sagittarius Sun and Aries Moon, who will be a lot of fun and very "type A", yet will have a flash temper, compared with someone with a Sagittarius Sun and Capricorn Moon, who will be more emotionally grounded and serious than many other Sagittarius Sun signs.

Here are a few things to consider to help you to make the most of your Sagittarius energy in different areas of life. Always consider that your soul chose

Sagittarius Strategies to Build Patience

Sagittarius means well, but they are often known for their lack of tact and "foot-in-mouth syndrome." Sagittarius also moves so fast that you may find it difficult to concentrate on what others are saying or their body language. The following strategies can help you slow down.

1. Develop active listening skills so that you are able to speak to people without bowling over them. To do this, "mirror" the other person mentally by slowing down and paying attention to their body language and repeating their words silently to yourself. This will help you gain some empathy and understanding for the other person.

2. Fast-moving Sagittarius won't find meditation easy since you generally don't like to sit still, but that makes it even more important. Sit comfortably and focus on your breath, saying to yourself, "Breathing in, breathing out," as you breathe. Try to let go of any other thoughts. You won't be able to let go of all of them, especially at first, but you will find that this will reduce thought clutter and make you calmer and less reactive. Do this daily for 10 to 15 minutes.

3. Take a walk. Walking calms the limbic system, which controls basic emotions, and also has the benefit of giving you time and space away from others and your everyday surroundings to sort through the multiple thoughts in your mind at any one time. A daily walk will get you far.

the Sagittarius energy so that you could be more independent and experiential in that area of life. You can choose to maximize the positive energies of Sagittarius.

GENERAL PERSONAL DEVELOPMENT

One issue that causes the most problems for Sagittarius is their lack of tact. Instead of offering a dogmatic opinion or whatever pops into your head, it can be very helpful to pause for a moment before speaking or asking questions. This pause will help you deliver what you have to say more tactfully.

RELATIONSHIPS/RELATING TO OTHERS

Sagittarius sits opposite to Gemini, the sign of the mind and perception, so it is good for Sagittarius to work on listening and perceiving more. This isn't to suggest that you should become completely like Gemini—only that you should infuse some of these qualities in your dealings with others to have more successful relationships.

ACHIEVING GOALS

Sagittarius is a mutable Fire sign that has no problem setting ambitious and audacious goals, but they do have issues sticking to what it takes to get there. Find support to help you complete the steps toward your goals and see them become a reality.

CAREERS

For a full analysis of what type of career you would be suited to, take into account the cusp of the tenth house (the Midheaven), the ruler of that sign, and any planets in the tenth house. For example, a person with Sagittarius Sun may have Scorpio on the cusp of the tenth house and Pluto (ruler of Scorpio) in the third house. This person might be suited to therapy or research positions (Scorpio in the tenth house), and either teaching or writing about their field of work (Pluto in the third house and Sagittarius Sun).

Jupiter and Sagittarius Journaling Exercise

Choose a quiet time and place to look at your natal chart. Identify Jupiter and Sagittarius in your chart. Look at the sign placement of Jupiter and the house placement of both Jupiter and Sagittarius. You can look at Sagittarius in the houses (see page 149) to get a feel for what Jupiter in the houses may also mean.

In your journal, write down keywords and phrases from this book and from your shamanic journey to Jupiter. Reflect on how you manifest these energies in your life and how you might choose to develop these energies in a more conscious rather than reactive way. For example, you may have Jupiter or Sagittarius in the sixth house and begin to understand that you are stifling your energy by trying to stick to rigid daily routines. With this awareness, you may decide to incorporate personal freedom into your life by varying your routines more often. Record your reflections in your journal.

Through this journaling exercise and your shamanic journey to Jupiter, you will begin to really understand the energies in your chart. Through that awareness, you will be able to choose *how* you embody the energies of Jupiter and Sagittarius in your life.

capricorn
the sea goat

It took me a lifetime. —PABLO PICASSO

Dates: December 20–January 20, depending on the year

ELEMENT	MODALITY	RULING PLANET	HOUSE RULED
Earth	Cardinal	Saturn	Tenth

Capricorn is a cardinal Earth sign and is ruled by Saturn. It's the tenth sign in the zodiac and is where we emerge onto the public stage and interact with the collective.

Capricorn is represented by the Sea Goat: a goat with the tail of a fish that represents a complexity sometimes missed when looking at Capricorn. The goat is a sure-footed creature that is always seeking new heights. Goats love to climb and stand on higher ground. Goats also teach us how to have trust in our own ability to land on our feet. The horns of the mountain goat, represented by the *V* in Capricorn's glyph, point to the future and also reflect the structural qualities of Capricorn. The tail of the fish symbolizes the fluid, intuitive side of Capricorn and is represented in the glyph by the curved tail on the horns or *V.*

Capricorn is practical, determined, persistent, ambitious, patient, loyal, and sensitive, with an underlying fear of inadequacy. Capricorn appears strong, disciplined, and controlled—always the authority figure and the keeper of boundaries and rules. Though Capricorn is all of that, the sensitivity of water that its tail represents means that Capricorn has a strong ethical presence. The watery energy also adds to their reserved and introverted nature. Capricorn likes to do the right thing in life and is the most honorable of signs.

Capricorn mellows with maturity and time once they feel that they have mastered a lot of what they came to master. An older Capricorn can be quite mischievous and less serious than a younger one. For example, someone with the Sun in Capricorn in the first house would be very reserved and even seem to be uptight. They would be concerned with their outer achievements and constantly need to prove themselves to the world (and themselves), but that impulse would lessen with age.

In an unaware state, Capricorn energy can be quite controlling and authoritarian. With awareness, Capricorn can choose to loosen this control and lighten up a little.

Now that you have a general feel for Capricorn energy, we'll look at *how* the planets show up in Capricorn and the houses. With your chart in hand, look for *which* planets you have in Capricorn, *how* the planets work in that sign, and *where* in the chart they are—the house. Then you will blend the energies by identifying keywords and phrases from all three that have meaning for you, remembering that you can replace them with any synonyms or phrases with the same meaning of your choosing. With this list, you will create a coherent and meaningful picture to get a deep understanding of how Capricorn energy manifests within you. This is where the real awareness and choice comes in. Armed with this knowledge, you can choose how you respond and react to Capricorn energy and how you choose to manifest it in the world.

PLANETS IN CAPRICORN

This section gives you a brief description of each planet in the sign Capricorn. I encourage you not to treat these discussions as definitive descriptions but as a springboard for your own interpretation using similar words and themes. You are invited to use these descriptions and the exercises in this chapter to create your own description of how the energies show up within you.

MOON IN CAPRICORN

The Moon represents your emotional body, and in Capricorn, you like a stable emotional life. However, this can make you feel a little cold at times because you dislike being drawn into emotional drama. You are cautious with emotional attachments but also very loyal once someone gains your trust. You are emotionally attached to outward proof of achievement. Being aware of this tendency can help you be more accepting of your own proof of everything you have achieved.

MERCURY IN CAPRICORN

Mercury represents communication and thought processes, and in Capricorn, you have a serious and practical mind with a great memory and ability to concentrate. Lack of material achievement brings worry for you as you prefer solidity and security. Tapping in to the more sensitive energies of Capricorn will help you develop a lighter frame of mind and more empathy for others.

VENUS IN CAPRICORN

Venus represents love, relationships, pleasure, creativity, and the value we place on the material things in life and our own pleasure. Venus in Capricorn needs reliable, consistent, and ambitious people to be in relationship with. If you have this placement, you prefer those who are more serious and traditional. You are drawn to more traditional and enduring art and ways of creating wealth. You are likely to have a strong relationship to your work.

MARS IN CAPRICORN

Mars represents your will, your drive, and your energy. With Mars in Capricorn, you are strong-willed, but you also have patience, which makes for a powerful combination. Be aware, however, that this pairing can be intimidating to others. Mars has the drive to start projects, and Capricorn has the determination to keep going, which makes you appear seemingly tireless. You are motivated by status and power as well as building wealth, but most of all, you desire to build something enduring in your life.

JUPITER IN CAPRICORN

Jupiter represents expansion, faith, truth, and freedom but also grandiosity. With Jupiter in Capricorn, you have great faith in yourself and the ability to actualize that faith and find good fortune in any chosen field as a result of your strength and integrity. Stability combined with optimism and patience makes Jupiter in Capricorn one of the most successful placements.

SATURN IN CAPRICORN

Saturn represents mastery, determination, and discipline. Saturn rules Capricorn, so this is a strong position for Saturn. If you have this placement, you are likely to be very hardworking and dedicated and find it difficult to take time to relax. You are inclined to naturally take the lead in projects, mainly because you have control over everything that way. Because Saturn rules Capricorn, and all the qualities of leadership and achievement are emphasized, this also means that the sensitive and fearful side of Capricorn is also enhanced. Be aware that you might find yourself fighting even harder for control due to that fear.

URANUS IN CAPRICORN

Uranus represents individuality, unpredictability, and unconventionality. Capricorn is conservative and concerned with rules and boundaries, so these two make an interesting and highly successful combination. As Capricorn works toward their goals, Uranus inspires innovation and inventiveness, along with diplomacy, which the stern Capricorn sometimes lacks.

NEPTUNE IN CAPRICORN

Neptune represents inspiration, illusion, psychic sensitivity, healing, and confusion. Neptune in Capricorn is the practical visionary who develops those visionary ideas slowly and steadily. If you have this placement, you can turn almost any dream into a practical application. Be aware, however, that you are a solitary worker who is prone to depression if things don't work out your way. Be mindful if any symptoms develop and seek help.

PLUTO IN CAPRICORN

Pluto is the soul or the soul's desire. Pluto spends approximately 20 years in each sign, so the mighty dwarf planet's influence is generational, which means that everyone in a generation is influenced by the sign that Pluto is in. The house placement must be blended with the generational concepts to get a clear picture for your own natal cosmic blueprint.

Pluto, at the time of this printing, is in Capricorn. This period began in 2008, continues to 2024 and will return in 2256. Those born with Pluto in Capricorn are a generation born to transform institutions and places of power. Since Capricorn is conservative, there may initially be internal resistance to change, but Pluto's ability to excavate that which is corrupt will compel this generation to transform. Napoleon, Beethoven, and former U.S. president Andrew Jackson were all born with Pluto in Capricorn.

SOUTH NODE IN CAPRICORN

If you have the South Node in Capricorn, you are learning to release the instinctive soul habit of needing to control everything and everyone. Your evolutionary lesson is to learn empathy and the ability to listen to and support others.

NORTH NODE IN CAPRICORN

If you have the North Node in Capricorn, you are learning the value of independence, self-respect, and becoming your own authority rather than being dependent on others. In other words, you are here to take charge of your own life.

Shamanic Journey to Saturn, Ruler of Capricorn

In this exercise, you are going to journey to non-ordinary reality, the upper world, in a practice called shamanic journey work. This is similar to a meditation but enables you to actively ask for guidance and answers. Shamanic journey work is an amazing practice for getting support in life. You can take a shamanic journey as often as you would like.

For this journey, search the term "Shamanic Drumming" on YouTube or your preferred video-streaming platform. Pick a track that is 10 to 15 minutes long. (I especially enjoy tracks by Shamanic Experience or Sandra Ingerman.) Experiment with two or three and decide which one feels right for you. It is best to listen using headphones or on high volume. Start the track once you have gotten comfortable.

Either lie on a comfortable blanket or sit comfortably with both feet on the ground. Start the track and close your eyes.

Picture yourself in a starting place. Mine is a meadow, but yours might be a beach, a mountain, a forest or any other place. Always trust what comes to you.

When you have pictured yourself in that place, look around to see if you have any spirit guides with you (commonly animals or other allies, which might include mythical creatures or even plants and trees). Ask your spirit guide(s) to journey with you. Next, look for a way to the upper world. It might be a ladder, stairs, or a beanstalk, or you may simply fly. Again, trust what comes to you.

Now imagine yourself journeying to Saturn, the ruler of Capricorn. Take note of everything that happens and have a conversation with Saturn by asking questions.

How can Saturn help you grow in the area of your chart where Saturn and/or Capricorn reside?

How can Saturn support you with your personal growth?

Saturn might respond by suggesting how you can learn to notice, express, and validate your feelings and insecurities honestly, or, alternatively, how you can learn to accept that others are less stoic and more emotional without judging and controlling them. Remember, this is a conversation where you are seeking to develop your energies in the best way possible for you.

When the conversation is over, thank Saturn and return to your starting place. When you are ready to open your eyes, journal about your experience.

CAPRICORN THROUGH THE HOUSES

The house where Capricorn falls in your natal chart brings deeper insights into those areas of life in which you exhibit leadership qualities and are the expert or authority. This is where you are naturally drawn to be more of a maker and follower of rules. Bring your awareness to how you might also be fearful and self-limiting in that area of life.

CAPRICORN IN THE FIRST HOUSE

If you have Capricorn in or on the cusp the first house, you are serious, mature, and responsible. You are reserved when people first meet you and seem almost shy, but this is really because you like to take your time to get to know people before letting them see behind your cool exterior. You have a strong presence, and others feel that they can lean on your strength.

CAPRICORN IN THE SECOND HOUSE

If you have Capricorn in or on the cusp of the second house, you have the ability to create a lot of wealth, especially through Capricorn-type fields of transformation, which can apply to personal, financial, or scientific fields. You will achieve a lot if you get clear about your own core values rather than focusing on other people's business.

CAPRICORN IN THE THIRD HOUSE

If you have Capricorn in or on the cusp of the third house, you are a person of few but effective words because you only like to say what needs to be said. You seem quiet and reserved because of this. You are a serious student and are prepared to put a lot of effort into that which you need to learn to achieve your goals, and once you feel proficient, you can become an authority on your chosen subject.

CAPRICORN IN THE FOURTH HOUSE

If you have Capricorn in or on the cusp of the fourth house, you may be late to building a family and home, and, when you do, it will have a traditional feel with you positioned as the responsible manager of the home. You may have difficulty getting in touch with your deepest feelings because of your attachment to tradition and rules, but once you do, you learn to set your own strong boundaries and rules.

CAPRICORN IN THE FIFTH HOUSE

Capricorn in or on the cusp of the fifth house doesn't find it easy to loosen up and have fun, especially in their youth, and their hobbies and pastimes will be related to work or will feel like work. However, Capricorn tends to loosen up with age, so your creativity may blossom when you are older. If you have children, you are a strict parent who takes on the role of teacher.

CAPRICORN IN THE SIXTH HOUSE

If you have Capricorn in or on the cusp of the sixth house, you need to be fulfilled at work or in daily life so that you don't feel as if you are wasting your time. If you are in that space, you are extremely self-disciplined, hardworking, and are likely to stay in that role for a long time. You may be attracted to work in governing institutions or entrepreneurship.

CAPRICORN IN THE SEVENTH HOUSE

Capricorn in or on the cusp of the seventh house indicates that you are attracted to a partner or significant other who is stable and who doesn't rush headlong into anything. You are supportive of others and demand the same from your significant relationships. Since you take all significant relationships very seriously, you may not commit to one person until you are older.

CAPRICORN IN THE EIGHTH HOUSE

If you have Capricorn in or on the cusp of the eighth house, you look to tradition in your search for truth in the mysteries of life and the deep psyche, preferring the tried-and-tested route rather than new approaches. In joint financial dealings, you prefer the same approach, and this is one arena where Capricorn may actually give away their power and entrust things to an external authority, which isn't necessarily a good thing. Try to be more self-trusting and open to new ideas.

CAPRICORN IN THE NINTH HOUSE

If you have Capricorn in or on the cusp of the ninth house, you are attracted to conventional beliefs that have been around a long time or will stick to the tradition you were brought up in. You are not a natural explorer and may travel only for work or to fulfill responsibilities. You prefer the places and history you know.

CAPRICORN IN THE TENTH HOUSE

If you have Capricorn in or on the cusp of the tenth house, the natural home of Capricorn, you are very career-oriented and may be a workaholic. You may be drawn to work in government or to work with older people. Capricorn is a slow and steady builder, and you may find great success at an older age after years of steady, determined, and practical progress.

CAPRICORN IN THE ELEVENTH HOUSE

If you have Capricorn in or on the cusp of the eleventh house, you have goals and ambition and are highly focused on working toward them. You are likely to choose friends from the organization where you work, and those friendships are very businesslike. As you mature, you are more likely to have a few closer bonded friendships.

CAPRICORN IN THE TWELFTH HOUSE

As Capricorn is all about the deeper realms of the psyche, if you have Capricorn in or on the cusp of the twelfth house, the house of the collective unconscious and connection to the muse and mystery, you are connected to the unconscious but often will not show it because it is not easily accepted in most traditional and conservative circles. You are, therefore, what could be described as a stealth intuitive, using your abilities in a practical way without sharing what you are doing. Be aware that this house increases the sensitive side of Capricorn, which can lead you to be reclusive.

CAPRICORN CASE STUDY

James has the following placements in his chart:

- Sun in Capricorn in the third house
- Moon in Aries in the sixth house
- Scorpio Ascendant

In this example, we are looking only at the Sun, Moon, and Ascendant, but the case study in Appendix A on page 213 integrates other elements in the natal chart.

James has deep-rooted fears of unworthiness and finds himself using his powerful presence to control others, and he overworks to mask his insecurities. Through his work with his natal chart, James has identified as a person who is an authoritative voice (Sun in the third house), a driven workaholic and natural leader (Aries Moon in the sixth house), and someone who comes across as extremely private but powerful (Scorpio Ascendant). With an Aries Moon in the sixth house and Scorpio Ascendant, James's third house Sun is more inclined to be a powerful leader, especially in the business world.

James's chart suggests that he use this awareness to learn to create a foundation of self-trust and self-respect by gently moving to the polarity point (Taurus) of his Ascendant. Since Taurus is very solid, like a tree, meditations that help James envision himself rooted like a tree with branches that reach out to others would be helpful.

THE SOUL IN CAPRICORN

The personality and behavior of Capricorn, or any Sun sign, is affected by all the other placements and aspects in the natal chart. This is why it is important to gradually blend the meanings of the planets, signs, houses, aspects, and transits to create an overall picture of the potential in your personal blueprint. If Capricorn is your Sun sign, you may have things in common with other Capricorn Sun signs, but you are uniquely you. For example, a Capricorn Sun with Pisces Ascendant will be extremely private and shy, whereas a Capricorn Sun with Aries Ascendant will be a natural leader. A person with a Capricorn Sun and Gemini Moon will be more sociable and communicative than someone

Capricorn Strategies to Notice and Validate Emotions

Capricorn has difficulty expressing their emotions because of their naturally reserved nature and lack of self-belief. The following strategies will help you learn to notice, validate, and then express your emotions in a way that suits you.

1. At the end of each day, sit down with your journal and write down all occasions where you have received positive feedback, however small. For example, this could mean your boss saying you did something well. You can also include past events in this exercise. If you struggle to think of events at first, use the time to list things you do well and that you are proud of yourself for. Treat this as a muscle-building exercise for your self-esteem. As it builds, you will find that your fear reduces, and you will be more able to express your vulnerable emotions.

2. Your patient and steady demeanor makes it second nature to pause from time to time. When you pause, check in with your gut. Emotions are often described as gut feelings, and if you pause and consciously ask your gut what it's feeling, you are more able to bring that sensitivity into your interactions with others.

3. Volunteer at a homeless shelter or a anywhere where assistance is needed. This will help you develop your emotional body while you are "working." Be sure to interact with the people you are helping—talk with them rather than performing your good service in silence.

with a Capricorn Sun and Virgo Moon, who will be very organized and married to their work.

Here are a few things to consider to help you to make the most of your Capricorn energy in different areas of life. Always consider that your soul chose the Capricorn energy so that you could be more determined and structured in that area of life. You can choose to maximize the positive energies of Capricorn.

GENERAL PERSONAL DEVELOPMENT

One issue that causes the most problems for Capricorn is their underlying fear that they are never enough, which tends to increase their shyness and difficulty expressing their emotions. Capricorn can benefit by reminding themselves that they are enough in any given moment with an affirmation such as "I am enough." Remember that everyone has a different knowledge base and that you don't have to know everything.

RELATIONSHIPS/RELATING TO OTHERS

Capricorn's opposite is Cancer, the sign of the mother, home, and your inner emotional life, so it is good for Capricorn to work on building a foundation of inner security. This isn't to suggest that you should become completely like Cancer—only that you should infuse some of these qualities in your dealings with others to have more successful relationships.

ACHIEVING GOALS

Capricorn is a cardinal Earth sign that is quite good at setting goals and working toward the completion of projects. Cardinal signs are less able to complete projects, and with Capricorn, it is the underlying fear of not being enough that often stops them from seeing them through. Remind yourself that "done" is better than "perfect" and move forward.

CAREERS

For a full analysis of what type of career you would be suited to, take into account the cusp of the tenth house (the Midheaven), the ruler of that sign, and any planets in the tenth house. For example, a person with a Capricorn Sun may have Sagittarius on the cusp of the tenth house and Jupiter (ruler of Sagittarius) in the second house. This person might be suited to teaching (Sagittarius in the tenth house) about financial matters (Jupiter in the second house) in the business arena (Capricorn Sun). Sagittarius on the Midheaven also suggests that this person would be best suited to a role that keeps them on the move rather than in one place.

Saturn and Capricorn Journaling Exercise

Choose a quiet time and place to look at your natal chart and have your journal handy. Identify Saturn and Capricorn in your chart. Look at the sign placement of Saturn and the house placement of both Saturn and Capricorn. You can look at Capricorn in the houses (see page 165) to get a feel for what Saturn in the houses may also mean.

In your journal, write down keywords and phrases from this book and from your shamanic journey to Saturn. Reflect on how you manifest these energies in your life and how you might choose to develop these energies in a more conscious rather than reactive way. For example, you may have Saturn or Capricorn in the twelfth house and realize that you have become reclusive to an unhealthy degree. With this awareness, you might choose to open yourself up to the outside world and be less afraid to share your sensitive, intuitive side. Record your reflections in your journal.

Through this journaling exercise, and your shamanic journey to Saturn, you will begin to really understand the energies in your chart. Through that awareness, you will be able to choose *how* you embody the energies of Saturn and Capricorn in your life.

aquarius the water-bearer

When a man is denied the right to live the life he believes in, he has no choice but to become an outlaw. —NELSON MANDELA

Dates: January 20–February 20, depending on the year

ELEMENT	MODALITY	RULING PLANET	HOUSE RULED
Air	Fixed	Uranus	Eleventh

Aquarius is a fixed Air sign and is ruled by Uranus, through the traditional ruler is Saturn. It's the eleventh sign in the zodiac and is where we find our tribe.

Aquarius is represented by the Water-Bearer—a figure pouring what seems to be water out of a vessel onto the earth. The complexity of this unique sign begins with this symbology. Some say it is water and, because the word *Aquarius* means "of water," that Aquarius is the forgotten Water sign. Others believe it is actually the spirit of the heavens being poured on the earth. The glyph for Aquarius is similarly complex as it is thought to be waves of water, electricity, or even two serpents symbolizing knowledge.

All of these descriptions reflect the complexity of the sign that is, in many ways, the most transpersonal. Aquarius has the energy of Air in that it represents connections beyond our physical selves, possessing knowledge that is otherworldly, original, inventive, and unique. This is the energy of thinking beyond our limits and making brand-new connections.

The modern and traditional rulers, Uranus and Saturn, respectively, also reflect the complexity of this sign. Aquarius, as a fixed sign, is often strangely conservative for such an inventive energy and is attracted to classical history, the ancient, and antiques. This is because Aquarius makes connections between all things and connects the dots between ancient influences and how they can be reinvented and integrated back into the modern world.

The key motivation for Aquarius is personal freedom and choosing their own path. Aquarius is socially conscious and questions authority; it is the energy of the benevolent rebel who wants equanimity and freedom for all and who honors diversity and difference. This is the sign of tribes in that it gathers people together who have similar values and goals. For example, someone with the Sun in Aquarius in the third house would be a highly inventive communicator and an "ideas person" whose mind is constantly on the go and heading down investigative rabbit holes.

In an unaware state, Aquarius energy can be unpredictable, emotionally distant, and even fanatical. With awareness, Aquarius can choose to make emotional connections within their communities, while still tempering their fanatic tendencies.

Now that you have a general feel for Aquarius energy, we'll look at *how* the planets show up in Aquarius and the houses. With your chart in hand, look for *which* planets you have in Aquarius, *how* the planets work in that sign, and *where* in the chart they are—the house. Then you will blend the energies by identifying keywords and phrases from all three that have meaning for you, remembering that you can replace them with any synonyms or phrases with the same meaning of your choosing. With this list, you will create a coherent and meaningful picture to get a deep understanding of how Aquarius energy manifests within you. This is where the real awareness and choice comes in. Armed with this knowledge, you can choose how you respond and react to Aquarius energy and how you manifest it in the world.

PLANETS IN AQUARIUS

This section gives you a brief description of each planet in the sign Aquarius. I encourage you not to treat these discussions as definitive descriptions but as a springboard for your own interpretation using similar words and themes. You are invited to use these descriptions and the exercises in this chapter to give you a description of how the energy of Aquarius and the planets show up within you.

MOON IN AQUARIUS

The Moon represents your emotional body, and in Aquarius, you are kind and compassionate. Though you are also emotionally detached, it is because your compassion is more about seeing the big picture. With Moon in Aquarius, you are friendly and will likely have friends who are considered outside the so-called norm. You are intellectually bright, generating unusual ideas, and you likely tend to be outside the norm, too.

MERCURY IN AQUARIUS

Mercury represents communication and thought processes, and in Aquarius, your mind works overtime and in overdrive. You quickly connect seemingly unconnected threads to create a big picture. In fact, with this placement, your mind is more inventive than any other placement. The fixed element of Aquarius can mean that you have extreme opinions at times and can stubbornly hold on to them. You do have a gift for tuning in to the ideas of the collective, even if it means you are likely to challenge those ideas.

VENUS IN AQUARIUS

Venus represents love, relationships, pleasure, creativity, and the value we place on the material things in life and our own pleasure. Venus in Aquarius is attracted to people who stimulate their mind and stir their innovative thoughts toward even more inventiveness. If you have this placement, you are generally open minded but actually quite intolerant of those you perceive to be selfish and those who put feelings over rationality. You are drawn to unusual and futuristic creative pursuits and art.

MARS IN AQUARIUS

Mars represents your will, your drive, and your energy. With Mars in Aquarius, you are likely to be a zealous reformer who drives change. It is often exhausting for others to be around all this energy. Your will is erratic and wired, and not many can keep up with it. For you, this can lead to frustration, resulting in becoming the anarchist or malcontent in the group. To avoid this, involve yourself in groups where your energy, inspiration, and innovation have an outlet.

JUPITER IN AQUARIUS

Jupiter represents expansion, faith, truth, and freedom but also grandiosity. Jupiter in Aquarius has a very expansive mind and is an explorer of ideas and possibilities that are fair and impartial. More than any other planet in Aquarius, you are likely to explore "alien" cultures both on and off the planet, and you are likely to break rules to get to the truth of things and create personal freedom.

SATURN IN AQUARIUS

Saturn represents mastery, determination, and discipline. Saturn is the traditional ruler of Aquarius and brings more of a conservative feel to the sometimes erratic and unpredictable Aquarian energy, which could be seen as a steadying influence that heightens the ability to focus and concentrate. If you have Saturn in Aquarius, you need more structure than most Aquarius placements, though that structure is likely to be slightly unconventional. Often loners, people with this placement can feel alone in a group and make few real friends. When you do make friends, you are extremely loyal.

URANUS IN AQUARIUS

Uranus represents individuality, unpredictability, and unconventionality. Aquarius is ruled by Uranus, making those with this placement the most unusual, unique, and unconventional people in the zodiac. If you have this placement, you are likely to be drawn to solving complex social problems like world poverty or world peace, or you may be drawn to working with computers, web technology, or any realm of math and science. Highly intelligent, you can come across as if you are looking down on those with lesser intellect, so keep this in mind when dealing with others.

NEPTUNE IN AQUARIUS

Neptune represents inspiration, illusion, psychic sensitivity, healing, and confusion. Neptune in Aquarius is highly creative and connected to both innovative ideas and the muse of inspiration. If you have this placement, it is likely you are perceived by others as having an otherworldly feel, which can make you appear aloof and seem like a dreamer.

PLUTO IN AQUARIUS

Pluto is the soul or the soul's desire. Pluto spends approximately 20 years in each sign, so the mighty dwarf planet's influence is generational, which means that everyone in a generation is influenced by the sign that Pluto is in. The house placement must be blended with the generational concepts to get a clear picture for your own natal cosmic blueprint.

Pluto was in Aquarius from 1778 to 1798 and will return in 2023. Those born with Pluto in Aquarius were part of a generation born to transform all of society in every field of life. Expect major innovations from the upcoming generation in areas of science, technology, social justice, and government institutions. Elizabeth I, Percy Bysshe Shelley, and Michael Faraday were all born with Pluto in Aquarius.

SOUTH NODE IN AQUARIUS

If you have the South Node in Aquarius, you are learning to release the instinctive soul habit of needing to fit in with others, which can make you susceptible to peer pressure. Your evolutionary lesson is to learn to follow your joy and heart's desires, which, of course, means knowing what those desires are.

NORTH NODE IN AQUARIUS

If you have the North Node in Aquarius, you are learning the value of championing group interests and relating to people as individuals rather than their position in life. You are also learning to see the bigger picture and participating in groups equally rather than needing to be the center of attention.

AQUARIUS THROUGH THE HOUSES

The house where Aquarius falls in your natal chart brings deeper insights into those areas of life in which you exhibit innovative and inventive qualities. This is where you are naturally drawn to be more rebellious and unpredictable.

Shamanic Journey to Uranus, Ruler of Aquarius

In this exercise you are going to journey to non-ordinary reality, the upper world, in a practice called shamanic journey work. This is similar to a meditation but enables you to actively ask for guidance and answers. Shamanic journey work is an amazing practice for getting support in life. You can take a shamanic journey as often as you would like.

For this journey, search the term "Shamanic Drumming" on YouTube or your preferred video-streaming platform. Pick a track that is 10 to 15 minutes long. (I especially enjoy tracks by Shamanic Experience or Sandra Ingerman.) Experiment with two or three and decide which one feels right for you. It is best to listen using headphones or on high volume. Start the track once you have gotten comfortable.

Either lie on a comfortable blanket or sit comfortably with both feet on the ground. Start the track and close your eyes.

Picture yourself in a starting place. Mine is a meadow, but yours might be a beach, a mountain, a forest or any other place. Always trust what comes to you.

When you have pictured yourself in that place, look around to see if you have any spirit guides with you (commonly animals or other allies, which might include mythical creatures or even plants and trees). Ask your spirit guide(s) to journey with you. Next, look for a way to the upper world. It might be a ladder, stairs, or a beanstalk, or you may simply fly. Again, trust what comes to you.

Now imagine yourself journeying to Uranus, the ruler of Aquarius. Take note of everything that happens and have a conversation with Uranus by asking questions.

How can Uranus help you grow in the area of your chart where Uranus and/or Aquarius reside?

How can Uranus support you with your personal growth?

Saturn might respond by suggesting how you can learn to take a few risks rather than following the herd, or, alternatively, how you can learn to accept and embrace a more childlike and playful quality on occasion. Remember, this is a conversation where you are seeking to develop your energies in the best way possible for you.

When the conversation is over, thank Uranus and return to your starting place. When you are ready to open your eyes, journal about your experience.

AQUARIUS IN THE FIRST HOUSE

If you have Aquarius in or on the cusp of the first house, you are seen as rebellious and unique. You help others see how things need to be changed and can show them what a different future can look like. More than anyone else, you want to be seen as different; you may have an unconventional look and dress uniquely. Others will be drawn to you to help solve problems and create innovative solutions.

AQUARIUS IN THE SECOND HOUSE

If you have Aquarius in or on the cusp of the second house, you are quite detached from the material world, and you may have an unstable financial and work life. However, your innovative mind may find unusual ways to make money. Your self-esteem and self-worth are more related to your ideas than creating wealth from them, and your reward would simply be the accomplishment of solving a complex problem. Your talent for identifying goals and connecting dots can be used to help others realize their dreams.

AQUARIUS IN THE THIRD HOUSE

If you have Aquarius in or on the cusp of the third house, you love learning and are very open to new ideas and ways to express yourself. You are forward thinking and would make a great teacher of any new ideas. Be aware, however, that your mind moves so fast that you are likely to be impatient with others and can speak without any awareness of the emotional impact it may have.

AQUARIUS IN THE FOURTH HOUSE

If you have Aquarius in or on the cusp of the fourth house, you may have had an unstable home life in your younger years and probably don't have very strong emotional ties to creating a family and stable home yourself. You may move a lot or even become a digital nomad in some way. If you do have a family of your own, you are fascinating and exciting to those you love, but be aware that if your children have an emotional need for stability, they may find your approach tough.

AQUARIUS IN THE FIFTH HOUSE

If you have Aquarius in or on the cusp of the fifth house, you often have unusual hobbies and pastimes because you like to do things in a radically different way from everyone else. You take your experimental approach into your love affairs, preferring to base those affairs on friendship. If you have children, you are an unconventional parent who will encourage your children to be independent and go their own way, even to the point of encouraging them to be rebellious.

AQUARIUS IN THE SIXTH HOUSE

If you have Aquarius in or on the cusp of the sixth house, you need to work in a team environment where there is variety and somewhere that's forward thinking and innovative. You would fit into the worlds of technology and science, especially if there is an element of inventiveness. You are happiest when your work is for the greater good of humanity.

AQUARIUS IN THE SEVENTH HOUSE

Aquarius in or on the cusp of the seventh house indicates that you are attracted to a partner or significant other who has common causes at heart and wants to be a part of something bigger, such as creating answers to the world's big problems. It's an uncomfortable placement for one-on-one relationships, as you want independence and for the other person to be an individual, but the more fixed quality of this energy may also lead you to want things your way. Learning give-and-take and true partnership is crucial here.

AQUARIUS IN THE EIGHTH HOUSE

If you have Aquarius in or on the cusp of the eighth house, you love to explore the world of the hidden, the metaphysical, and the psychological, and you investigate the connections that show why and how things work. You are drawn to figuring out answers to the deepest of mysteries in your search for truth. In more mundane matters, you like unconventional approaches to joint financial dealings, perhaps making unusual investments.

AQUARIUS IN THE NINTH HOUSE

If you have Aquarius in or on the cusp of the ninth house, you are a rebel against the belief systems that have been imposed on you as you reject any dogma that isn't from you. You are open to many beliefs and can see the threads and connections that join them all together. You enjoy being around people who challenge long-held beliefs. You apply the same ethos to travel and exploration of other cultures.

AQUARIUS IN THE TENTH HOUSE

If you have Aquarius in or on the cusp of the tenth house, you are drawn to make a public contribution to humanitarian and/or social causes and are able to use your innovative ideas to come up with new ways to help others. You are unlikely to enjoy when others try to have authority over you and how you do things due to your need for personal freedom; therefore, you may be drawn to entrepreneurship so that you can work within a group or organization without working for them. You do not, however, like being the public face of such groups.

AQUARIUS IN THE ELEVENTH HOUSE

If you have Aquarius in or on the cusp of the eleventh house, the natural house of Aquarius, you are likely to have large groups of eccentric and unusual friends. This is the realm of the alternative-lifestyle groups and the rebels of society, those who don't fit into the conventions that society imposes on people. You are likely to be quite tech savvy and could be involved in groups that connect through the internet rather than in person.

AQUARIUS IN THE TWELFTH HOUSE

As Aquarius is all about originality and inventiveness, if you have Aquarius in or on the cusp of the twelfth house, the house of the collective unconscious and connection to the muse and mystery, you are connected to the unconscious in your own unique way. Your ability to make connections others don't see helps you get in touch with the spiritual side of your humanitarian nature in a way that others are unable to do.

AQUARIUS CASE STUDY

Jackie has the following placements in her chart:

- Sun in Aquarius in the second house
- Moon in Aries in the fourth house
- Sagittarius Ascendant

In this example, we are looking only at the Sun, Moon, and Ascendant, but the case study in Appendix A on page 213 integrates other elements in the natal chart.

Jackie finds it really difficult to make strong emotional connections to others and tends to be really hard on herself at times. Through her work with her natal chart, Jackie identifies as a freedom-loving entrepreneur (Sun in the second house) who may like living alone or having her home the way she likes it (Aries Moon in the fourth house) and who loves to be out and about and is very fun loving (Sagittarius Ascendant). With an Aries Moon in the fourth house and Sagittarius Ascendant, Jackie's second house Sun is even more freedom loving than the Aquarius Sun alone indicates, and she may have moved a lot and be very independent.

Jackie's chart suggests that she will benefit from doing some deep work to help her connect with her own emotions first and then learn to slow down and connect to the emotions of those she cares about.

THE SOUL IN AQUARIUS

The personality and behavior of Aquarius, or any Sun sign, is affected by all the other placements and aspects in the natal chart. This is why it is important to gradually blend the meanings of the planets, signs, houses, aspects, and transits to create an overall picture of the potential in your personal blueprint.

If Aquarius is your Sun sign, you may have things in common with other Aquarius Sun signs, but you are uniquely you. For example, an Aquarius Sun with Capricorn Ascendant will be more grounded but also quite conservative, whereas an Aquarius Sun with Scorpio Ascendant will be extremely private and

Aquarius Strategies to Have More Fun and Connect with Others

Aquarius has their head in the clouds because they are mentally connecting dots on a constant basis; this means they often find it difficult to have fun and connect with other people. The following strategies can help you learn to have fun and build connections.

1. Go to a playground and play on the swings once a week for a half hour. Feel the earth beneath your feet as you push off, and feel the wind in your hair as you swing. Close your eyes, feeling the pure joy of having fun.

2. Do heart-opening meditations to connect with others at more than an intellectual level. Simple, guided heart-opening meditations can easily be found by searching "heart-opening meditation" on your favorite video- or audio-streaming platform.

3. Join an intuitive painting class or group. Intuitive painting is a process that channels the inner child, and it is often suggested that you paint with your nondominant hand. It's a highly creative practice that involves no planning, training, or analysis and is focused on the process rather than the results. Its aim is to free you from the mind and paint only what makes you feel good or happy.

probably work in deep research. Another example is a person with an Aquarius Sun and Sagittarius Moon, who may teach what they know or be a digital nomad, compared with someone with an Aquarius Sun and Taurus Moon, who will be more connected to the material world than most.

Here are a few things to consider to help you to make the most of your Aquarius energy in different areas of life. Always consider that your soul chose the Aquarius energy so that you could be more socially conscious and inventive in that area of life. You can choose to maximize the positive energies of Aquarius.

GENERAL PERSONAL DEVELOPMENT

One issue that causes the most problems for Aquarius is their unpredictability, because others find they are not easy to rely on. Taken to the extreme, this can mean that people will stop counting on you for anything. Practice following through on commitments to bring more connection and trust from the people in your life.

RELATIONSHIPS/RELATING TO OTHERS

Looking opposite from Aquarius we find Leo, the sign of the heart, enthusiasm, confidence, and individuality, so it is good for Aquarius to work on being willing to step forward into the spotlight now and again. This isn't to suggest that you should become completely like Leo—only that you should infuse some of these qualities in your dealings with others to have more successful relationships.

ACHIEVING GOALS

Aquarius is very future oriented, so they have big plans and set audacious goals. Their erratic and contrary behavior, however, can mean they quickly move from one project to another. Tap in to the stubborn side of your nature to see a goal through to fruition.

CAREERS

For a full analysis of what type of career you would be suited to, take into account the cusp of the tenth house (the Midheaven), the ruler of that sign, and any planets in the tenth house. For example, a person with an Aquarius Sun may have Libra on the cusp of the tenth house and Uranus (ruler of Aquarius) in the second house. This person might be suited for work involving diplomacy and mediation (Libra in the tenth house) about financial matters (Uranus in the second house), and that gives them the opportunity to think outside the box to resolve problems (Aquarius Sun).

Uranus and Aquarius Journaling Exercise

Choose a quiet time and place to look at your natal chart and have your journal handy. Identify Uranus and Aquarius in your chart. Look at the sign placement of Uranus and the house placement of both Uranus and Aquarius. You can look at Aquarius in the houses (see page 177) to get a feel for what Uranus in the houses may also mean.

In your journal, write down keywords and phrases from this book and from your shamanic journey to Uranus. Reflect on how you manifest these energies in your life and how you might choose to develop these energies in a more conscious rather than reactive way. For example, you may have Uranus or Aquarius in the fifth house and realize that you aren't expressing your unconventionality in your hobbies. With this awareness, you might choose to take up studying astrology, a very Aquarian activity, for example, and do so in your own unique way. Record your reflections in your journal.

Through this journaling exercise and your shamanic journey to Uranus, you will begin to really understand the energies in your chart. Through that awareness, you will be able to choose *how* you embody the energies of Uranus and Aquarius in your life.

pisces the fishes

The timeless in you is aware of life's timelessness. And knows that yesterday is but today's memory and tomorrow is today's dream. —KAHLIL GIBRAN, *THE PROPHET*

Dates: February 20–March 20, depending on the year

ELEMENT	MODALITY	RULING PLANET	HOUSE RULED
Water	Mutable	Neptune	Twelfth

Pisces is a mutable Water sign and is ruled by Neptune. It's the twelfth and last sign of the zodiac and is a culmination of all the signs. Pisces is where we merge with the oneness of all that is.

Pisces is represented by the Fish (actually two fish tied together swimming in opposite directions). The glyph is two crescent moons joined by a line. The crescent moon represents the darkest time of the moon—the most mystical, mysterious, and magical—when we go within to set intentions for the beginning of each lunar cycle. The Fish represents feelings, deep awareness, fertility, birth and rebirth, and the unconscious or higher self. All of this is represented by Pisces.

Like water, the moon, and fish, Pisces is sensitive to vibrations, receptive, and fluid. The fluidity of Pisces and the duality of the Fish as they swim in different directions between the spirit and material worlds represent different ideas, different people, different things, imagination and deception, the manifest and the spiritual.

Pisces is imaginative, intuitive, compassionate, empathic, and dreamy. Pisces is also spiritual and mystical but prone to illusion, escapism, and possibly even addictions. This is the most transcendent of signs—and can be the most despondent at times, as they can feel disillusioned with things or plunge themselves into self-sacrifice. Pisces is a highly creative energy that has visions and enjoys the realms of fantasy and imagination. For example, the Sun in Pisces in the fifth house would be a playful and imaginative creator but may swim in the seas of indecision about exactly what they desire to create.

In an unaware state, Pisces energy can be hypersensitive and lack boundaries, which can mean they take on savior or martyr roles. They are also prone to escapism of all kinds, and some of those pursuits are healthier than others. The realms of fantasy through film or other art, for example, would be a better choice than alcohol or drugs. Pisces needs time to dream and imagine, so learning to choose healthy ways to do that is crucial.

Now that you have a general feel for Pisces, we'll look at *how* the planets show up in Pisces and the houses. With your chart in hand, look for *which* planets you have in Pisces, *how* the planets work in that sign, and *where* in the chart they are—the house. Then you will blend the energies by identifying keywords and phrases from all three that have meaning for you, remembering that you can replace them with any synonyms or phrases with the same meaning of your choosing. With this list, you will create a coherent and meaningful picture to get a deep understanding of how this energy manifests within you. This is where the real awareness and choice comes in. Armed with this knowledge, you can choose how you respond and react to Pisces energy and how you manifest it in the world.

PLANETS IN PISCES

This section gives you a brief description of each planet in the sign Pisces. I encourage you not to treat these discussions as definitive descriptions but as a springboard for your own interpretation using similar words and themes. You are invited to use these descriptions and the exercises in this chapter to create your own description of how the energy of Pisces and the planets show up within you.

MOON IN PISCES

The Moon represents your emotional body, and in Pisces, which also has watery, lunar qualities, you are highly sensitive, intuitive, and receptive. In fact, you may be a psychic sponge and have to find tools to help you differentiate your own feelings from the feelings of the collective. You are very sensitive to the atmosphere and can even feel ill if the environment doesn't support you. Inspiration is divine for this placement and will fuel everything you do, especially your creativity.

MERCURY IN PISCES

Mercury represents communication and thought processes, and in Pisces, you have the vivid imagination of a storyteller in some way. You are a natural channel, and words come through you, not from you. Similarly, you learn by osmosis and absorb information through perceptions. You seem as if you are in a dream a lot of the time, because you are! You may find handling details challenging and be rather naive and unfocused, but if you stick to creative pursuits, you will be in your element.

VENUS IN PISCES

Venus represents love, relationships, pleasure, creativity, and the value we place on the material things in life and our own pleasure. Venus in in Pisces is the most romantic of placements, and they see everything through rose-colored glasses. If you have this placement, you are highly sensitive to the needs of those you love and will do almost anything to attend to their needs. This placement is the epitome of *agape,* the highest form of love. Because you love unconditionally, this can open you up to illusion and deception from those with less-than-pure motives, so try to remember to take off your rose-colored glasses on occasion.

MARS IN PISCES

Mars represents your will, your drive, and your energy. In Pisces, energy is dispersed and fluid, which is a frustrating place for Mars. If you have this placement, you are sensitive and vulnerable and need a creative outlet for your drive because it really doesn't know where to direct itself. Not knowing what you want can be a difficult thing for Mars energy and make you prone to sudden shifts of emotion. You are likely to be creatively gifted, so find solid avenues to explore your creativity to put Mars at ease.

JUPITER IN PISCES

Jupiter represents expansion, faith, truth, and freedom but also grandiosity. Jupiter in Pisces is one of the most empathic and charitable placements in the zodiac. They are fabulous listeners who love to help others. This placement has a big healing energy that others are drawn to, and they make fabulous counselors. Jupiter expands everything it touches, so if you have this placement, you have a big imagination and a colorful, rich dream life. Because you see the world as full of possibilities, you tend toward escapist behaviors if confronted with less-than-savory aspects of the world.

SATURN IN PISCES

Saturn represents mastery, determination, and discipline. Saturn in Pisces can often be fearful and self-conscious as Saturn restricts the imaginative and spiritual qualities of Pisces. There's a feeling of always wanting to do the right thing that can bring you to see what might go wrong rather than being open to possibilities, and you can be prone to depression. If you have this placement, learn to trust your strong intuition and allow your imagination to flow in order to help you move beyond some of the fearfulness. If you notice any symptoms of depression, seek help.

URANUS IN PISCES

Uranus represents individuality, unpredictability, and unconventionality. Uranus in Pisces has a boundless and unconventional imagination that is visionary to the extreme. This placement is highly attuned to both the collective unconscious and energies beyond this world. If you have this placement, you thrive when using your abilities to dream up ways to help people on a grand scale, but if your mind and imagination aren't kept busy, you can feel lethargic and sad, so be sure to keep Uranus in Pisces engaged.

NEPTUNE IN PISCES

Neptune represents inspiration, illusion, psychic sensitivity, healing, and confusion. Neptune in the sign of its rulership is mystical, psychic, and lives by inspiration. This is the energy of those who sacrifice themselves for others to the degree that when they actually need help from others, it's willingly given to these inspirational folk. With Neptune in Pisces, you are very spiritual and live in a state of heightened consciousness or, conversely, can be prone to escapism and addiction. Be aware of these tendencies so that you can seek any assistance needed.

PLUTO IN PISCES

Pluto is the soul or the soul's desire. Pluto spends approximately 20 years in each sign, so the mighty dwarf planet's influence is generational, which means that everyone in a generation is influenced by the sign that Pluto is in. The house placement must be blended with the generational concepts to get a clear picture for your own natal cosmic blueprint.

Pluto was in Pisces from 1797 to 1823 and will return in 2044. Those born with Pluto in Pisces were a generation of people who delved deeply into psychic abilities and collective secrets. There may have been increased use of psychotropic drugs during this period and in this generation, as this placement wishes to explore the unconscious, and it is believed that these substances open the doors of perception. Abraham Lincoln, William Shakespeare, Edgar Allan Poe, and Karl Marx were all born with Pluto in Pisces.

SOUTH NODE IN PISCES

If you have the South Node in Pisces, you are learning to release the instinctive soul habits of overgiving and selflessness. You are constantly looking to help others by seeking fairness and justice, but you rarely look after yourself. Once you realize that you are more able to truly help others when you care for yourself, you will be more fulfilled.

NORTH NODE IN PISCES

If you have the North Node in Pisces, you are learning the value of compassion, trust, and surrender. You are born with a compulsive need to control everything in your life, which leads to perfectionism in an ever-changing world. Spiritual practices such as meditation and prayer help build trust that the universe will unfold in a way that is better than you can control.

Shamanic Journey to Neptune, Ruler of Pisces

In this exercise, you are going to journey to non-ordinary reality, the upper world, in a practice called shamanic journey work. This is similar to a meditation but enables you to actively ask for guidance and answers. Shamanic journey work is an amazing practice for getting support in life. You can take a shamanic journey as often as you would like.

For this journey, search the term "Shamanic Drumming" on YouTube or your preferred video-streaming platform. Pick a track that is 10 to 15 minutes long. (I especially enjoy tracks by Shamanic Experience or Sandra Ingerman.) Experiment with two or three and decide which one feels right for you. It is best to listen using headphones or on high volume. Start the track once you have gotten comfortable.

Either lie on a comfortable blanket or sit comfortably with both feet on the ground. Start the track and close your eyes.

Picture yourself in a starting place. Mine is a meadow, but yours might be a beach, a mountain, a forest, or any other place. Always trust what comes to you.

When you have pictured yourself in that place, look around to see if you have any spirit guides with you (commonly animals or other allies, which might include mythical creatures or even plants and trees). Ask your spirit guide(s) to journey with you. Next, look for a way to the upper world. It might be a ladder, stairs, or a beanstalk, or you may simply fly. Again, trust what comes to you.

Now imagine yourself journeying to Neptune, the ruler of Pisces. Take note of everything that happens and have a conversation with Neptune by asking questions.

How can Neptune help you grow in the area of your chart where Neptune and/or Pisces reside?

How can Neptune support you with your personal growth?

Neptune might respond by suggesting how you can learn to put yourself first some of the time, or, alternatively, how you can learn to develop your individuality. Remember, this is a conversation where you are seeking to develop your energies in the best way possible for you.

When the conversation is over, thank Neptune and return to your starting place. When you are ready to open your eyes, journal about your experience.

PISCES THROUGH THE HOUSES

The house where Pisces falls in your natal chart brings deeper insights into those areas of life in which you exhibit compassion and selflessness. This is where you are naturally drawn to be more focused on the spiritual pathway.

PISCES IN THE FIRST HOUSE

If you have Pisces in or on the cusp of the first house, you are seen as shy and unsure of yourself. It can be difficult for others to see the real you behind the fluid and receptive nature that they witness soaking up the energy of those around them; others see someone who seems to have their head in the clouds. You are empathic, sensitive, and creative and can express your visionary self best through art.

PISCES IN THE SECOND HOUSE

If you have Pisces in or on the cusp of the second house, you may find budgeting and tracking of finances difficult because you find focus and commitment hard, preferring to swim with the tide. You are naturally generous, however, and this openness can attract fortune. You are spiritually connected to the natural world and can probably receive spiritual messages from that connection. You may attract money through your use of your intuitive and creative abilities.

PISCES IN THE THIRD HOUSE

If you have Pisces in or on the cusp of the third house, you learn best by osmosis rather than through structured learning; you may spend time in the classroom dreaming. Once you accept that this is how you learn, you can immerse yourself in a subject, and your receptive nature will soak up the information. You probably learn best when alone so that you aren't distracted by what everyone else is thinking about. When you communicate from your soul and not just your mind, your words are powerful, but if you try to think too hard about what you are saying, your message is confused.

PISCES IN THE FOURTH HOUSE

If you have Pisces in or on the cusp of the fourth house, your home needs to be a safe haven and peaceful; otherwise, you will find yourself retreating into your own world. You need support and stability from your family, but you may not be able to see them clearly for who they are. Be aware that too much activity and noise in your home drains you energetically.

PISCES IN THE FIFTH HOUSE

If you have Pisces in or on the cusp of the fifth house, you need creative hobbies that allow full expression of your feelings and intuitive abilities—stream-of-consciousness writing or intuitive painting, for example. You may also be drawn to film or television. You have a tendency to be selfless with any children you have, but be aware that you may give them too much. When it comes to love, you may be attracted to people who need saving.

PISCES IN THE SIXTH HOUSE

If you have Pisces in or on the cusp of the sixth house, you are more suited to work as an employee with someone to guide you, but be wary of anyone who might want to take advantage of your gentle nature. You need work that is spiritually fulfilling and where you feel you are helping others. Your physical health may suffer if you are not in meaningful or fulfilling work.

PISCES IN THE SEVENTH HOUSE

Pisces in or on the cusp of the seventh house indicates that you are attracted to a partner or significant who brings connection to the spiritual world and creativity into your life to help you open up to new experiences. You need someone who is sensitive and can soothe your feelings. You will be the one who takes care of details and organization in these relationships.

PISCES IN THE EIGHTH HOUSE

If you have Pisces in or on the cusp of the eighth house, you are drawn to exploring the deepest realms of the unconscious and may even be drawn to mediumship. You are also inclined to being extremely self-sacrificing in your bonded relationships, which can open you up to feeling disempowered and losing any sense of self. It is even more important that you learn to listen to and trust your own intuition here so that you don't give all of yourself away to others.

PISCES IN THE NINTH HOUSE

If you have Pisces in or on the cusp of the ninth house, spiritual or religious beliefs are very important to you. You tend to be drawn to the more transcendent forms of belief, such as Buddhism, Sufism, or any of the other mystical traditions. You may also be drawn to spending time in religious communities. You find guidance through these practices. If you travel, you are often drawn to water.

PISCES IN THE TENTH HOUSE

If you have Pisces in or on the cusp of the tenth house, you may have challenges deciding exactly what your path in life is because you are, in your soul, a visionary who doesn't really fit into a particular role. You are at your best if you follow your desire to help others in a spiritual or metaphysical way or engage in work that embraces your amazing imagination.

PISCES IN THE ELEVENTH HOUSE

If you have Pisces in or on the cusp of the eleventh house, you are an extremely generous friend but may give more than you have in terms of money and self. You are drawn to more spiritually based groups of friends and organizations, but you could also benefit from surrounding yourself with some more grounded friends. You have idealistic dreams and goals.

PISCES IN THE TWELFTH HOUSE

As Pisces is all about spiritual connection, if you have Pisces in or on the cusp of the twelfth house, the house of the collective unconscious and connection to the muse and mystery, you have an otherworldly connection to the mystical and magical realms. You also have deep levels of empathy that can lead to a general feeling of sadness for humanity. You probably love to spend a lot of time alone.

PISCES CASE STUDY

Edward has the following placements in his chart:

- Sun in Pisces in the tenth house
- Moon in Cancer in the second house
- Gemini Ascendant

In this example, we are looking only at the Sun, Moon, and Ascendant, but the case study in Appendix A on page 213 integrates other elements in the natal chart.

Edward often feels "stuck in the mud" and unable to take action as he is, at his core, a dreamer despite his seemingly sociable persona (Gemini Ascendant). Through working with his natal chart, he identifies as a creative visionary (Sun in the tenth house) who may be a body healer such as a massage therapist (Cancer Moon in the second house) and who loves to teach and communicate what he knows (Gemini Ascendant). Both the Pisces Sun in the tenth house and the Cancer Moon in the second house are watery planets in Earth houses, though he has an emotional or spiritual connection to nature. The Gemini Ascendant will lighten the "muddy" nature of the Water-Earth combination.

Edward's chart suggests that he find ways to inspire and fire up his passions, perhaps by focusing on building relationships with fiery people in his life (his Sagittarius Descendant, the polarity of his Ascendant) who will help pull him out of the muddiness.

THE SOUL IN PISCES

The personality and behavior of Pisces, or any Sun sign, is affected by all the other placements and aspects in the natal chart. This is why it is important to gradually blend the meanings of the planets, signs, houses, aspects, and transits to create an overall picture of the potential in your personal blueprint.

If Pisces is your Sun sign, you may have things in common with other Pisces Sun signs, but you are uniquely you. For example, a Pisces Sun with Scorpio Ascendant will be private and seem to be able to read another's soul and mind, whereas a Pisces Sun with Capricorn Ascendant will be more grounded and will have more of an idea about what they want to achieve in life. Another example is a person with a Pisces Sun and Aquarius Moon who will more easily be able

Pisces Strategies to Increase Connection with the Real World

Pisces have a big tendency toward escapism. They have trouble dealing with the real world due to being so empathic to all the energies around them. The following strategies will help you manage that energy and connect with reality.

1. Grounding techniques bring you back into the present moment and bring your awareness to the physical world around you. Take an inventory of everything around you with all your senses: identify colors and patterns, count objects and touch them, and smell and listen to your environment. Become hypersensitive to all that you notice in the moment. This will connect you to the world around you.

2. A simple grounding technique that can be done anywhere is to sit on a chair (or it can be done standing if needed) with both feet flat on the floor. Make a mental note of the feeling of your body on the chair and/or your feet on the ground. Cross your arms over your chest and gently tap your shoulders, alternating one at a time. If you are in public, you can tap your thighs one leg at a time. The tapping brings your attention back to your body and into the present.

3. When you are feeling very sensitive, draw yourself a warm bath, and put Epsom salts or mineral salts in the water. Soak in the tub for a while to calm yourself and help you feel like you are in your element. Do this weekly or whenever the need arises.

to detach from their strong empathic abilities and not take on everyone else's feelings than someone with a Pisces Sun and Leo Moon, who will be more comfortable in the spotlight and more playfully creative.

Here are a few things to consider to help you to make the most of your Pisces energy in different areas of life. Always consider that your soul chose Pisces energy so that you could be more compassionate and intuitive in that area of life. You can choose to maximize the positive energies of Pisces.

GENERAL PERSONAL DEVELOPMENT

One issue that causes the most problems for Pisces is their tendency to withdraw from the real world, which is a form of escapism. Their evolutionary path is to integrate the spirit realm into the physical world so that they can fully interact with other people and groups. You will find additional meaning in life by getting out into the world.

RELATIONSHIPS/RELATING TO OTHERS

Opposite of Pisces is Virgo, the sign of service to others and hand skills and talents, so it is good for Pisces to focus on service and taking up a skill that requires them to use their hands to focus more on the physical world. This isn't to suggest that you should become completely like Virgo—only that you should infuse some of these qualities in your dealings with others to have more successful relationships.

ACHIEVING GOALS

Pisces has great difficulty knowing what their goals are as they are always swimming between different ideas or will often dream about the end product but not do the work. Either way, their dreams and goals are big and idealistic. You may be just happy dreaming about your goals, but if you want to actually achieve them, you may require support.

CAREERS

For a full analysis of what type of career you would be suited to, take into account the cusp of the tenth house (the Midheaven), the ruler of that sign, and any planets in the tenth house. For example, a person with a Pisces Sun may have Taurus on the cusp of the tenth house and Venus (ruler of Taurus) in the seventh house. This person might be suited to work that involves nature or the body (Taurus in the tenth house) or working with relationships (Venus in the seventh house) in a creative capacity (Pisces Sun).

Neptune and Pisces Journaling Exercise

Choose a quiet time and place to look at your natal chart and have your journal handy. Identify Neptune and Pisces in your chart. Look at the sign placement of Neptune and the house placement of both Neptune and Pisces. You can look at Pisces in the houses (see page 193) to get a feel for what Neptune in the houses may also mean.

In your journal, write down keywords and phrases from this book and from your shamanic journey to Neptune. Reflect on how you manifest these energies in your life and how you might choose to develop these energies in a more conscious rather than reactive way. For example, you may have Neptune or Pisces in the fourth house and realize that your home needs to be a more peaceful space. With this awareness, you might choose to move to a more peaceful location or rearrange or redecorate your home (or part of it) to imbue it with an air of peace. Record your reflections in your journal.

Through this journaling exercise and your shamanic journey to Neptune, you will begin to really understand the energies in your chart. Through that awareness, you will be able to choose *how* you embody the energies of Neptune and Pisces in your life.

CHAPTER FIFTEEN

working with aspects

Aspects are the relationships between the planets and angles in a natal chart; they represent how the planets work together in the chart. Aspects are described as harmonic, dynamic, or neutral, but the nature of the planets involved must also be taken into account. There are no good or bad aspects; some bring more tension but also more impetus for change and growth. Some are more harmonious, but the opportunities they present can be missed due to a lack of tension. As always, your personal approach and commitment to growth is what really counts.

Aspects are measured as angles within the ecliptic circle with a margin of "play" called orbs (see the sidebar on page 202). This means that the angle can be within a few degrees of exact. For example, a square aspect (90°) would still be in play at 85° or 95°. For instance, Mars at 12° Aquarius would be square to the Moon at 17° Taurus even though both planets are not at the same degree. I am only going to discuss the major aspects, the Ptolemaic aspects, because there is more than enough information contained within these aspects for you to be able to integrate the energies for personal growth. I suggest you master the integration of these major aspects before diving into minor aspects.

In case you find it difficult to work with angular math, the table on page 205 will help you identify which aspects to look for in your chart. Also, refer back to the sample chart on page 15, which labels the aspects to help you visualize the angles. Later in the chapter, I explain how to identify aspects. I suggest you read through the following explanatory material, but do not worry too much right now about how to identify them. You can later reread this material with a better understanding.

THE ASPECTS

The aspects discussed in this section are the primary aspects used in astrology with suggested orbs. The elements of the signs that the planets are in are very helpful for understanding the aspects.

CONJUNCTION  —0°

ORBS: Sun, Moon, Jupiter, and Saturn up to 10°; all other planets 5° to 7°

The conjunction is generally a harmonious aspect, depending on the energies involved. The conjunction amplifies the energies of both planets, the sign they are in, and the element of the sign as the planets are conjunct in the same sign and element. A Mercury/Uranus conjunction in Leo, for example, combines Air (Mercury and Uranus rule the Air signs Gemini and Aquarius) with Fire (Leo). Air fans the flames of Fire, so this combination means this person has an active and creative mind.

Orbs

In astrology, the orb is how much an angle made by two points differs from the exactness of an aspect. There are different opinions regarding how wide orbs can be, and I encourage you to use your intuition once you understand your chart and the aspects. For example, a 12° Gemini Moon opposing a Sagittarius stellium (three or more planets in the same sign) with the stellium at 0°, 7°, 14°, and 21° would mean that the Moon would be considered to oppose all the Sagittarius planets, even though the orb is wider than might usually be the case for the planet at 0°. That planet is pulled into opposition by the other planets in a stellium. Orbs are wider depending on the strength of the planet.

The Sun and Moon will have a wider orb than other planets. The smaller the orb, or the closer to the same degree the planets are, the more powerful the aspect.

However, with a Mars/Neptune conjunction, for example, the fluid, dissolving energy of Neptune (ruler of the Water sign Pisces) can weaken the drive and energy of Mars (ruler of the Fire sign Aries), but the person will also have an extremely active imagination and be quite magnetic to others.

Planets very close to the Sun are said to combust within 3°. This means that the energy of the Sun overwhelms the other planet and burns it out so its energy is weakened.

OPPOSITION   ⚬⚬   −180°

ORBS: Sun, Moon, Jupiter, and Saturn up to 10°; all other planets 5° to 7°

An opposition is a dynamic aspect with the tension of opposites. Traditionally, this is seen as a difficult aspect, but much of this depends on the planets involved in the opposition. The opposition often has a motivating and invigorating effect that moves you into action, as the opposition always involves elements that blend well (if consciously integrated) and can usually bring positive results, even if getting there is not always easy. For example, Earth and Water can be integrated to mold or sculpt something concrete, and Air fans the flames of Fire, as discussed earlier.

The planet, house, sign, and elements should all be taken into account when integrating the meaning of an opposition—for example, the Moon (Water) in Gemini (Air) in the sixth house (Earth as naturally ruled by Virgo) opposing Jupiter (Fire, ruler of Sagittarius) in Sagittarius (Fire) in the twelfth house (Water as naturally ruled by Pisces). This suggests that this person has big (Jupiter) highs and lows emotionally (mutable Gemini and Sagittarius) and that they are so connected to messages from the collective unconscious (twelfth house) that they translate practically for others (sixth house service).

SQUARE   ☐   −90°

ORBS: Sun, Moon, Jupiter, and Saturn up to 10°; all other planets 5° to 7°

The square is the most challenging aspect; the energies are quite literally squaring off, which means preparing for a battle. Picture the planets in a square as being on the defensive and ready to fight. The key, of course, is to learn to integrate the two energies so that they work together rather than letting them move in two different directions.

For example, a Mars/Pluto square provides a lot of drive and energy to assert dominance, but that is likely to lead to aggressive assertiveness toward others if this person feels that others are blocking them in any way. If this were the case for you, one way to manage this very powerful square is to dial in your ambition and energy to stay highly focused on your own goals and to return anything you see as blocks by others to the sender with consciousness—in other words, do not allow yourself to be affected by other people's views.

SEXTILE ✳ −30°

ORBS: all planets generally up to 5°

The sextile aspect is one of opportunity. It's a harmonious aspect where the energies work well together, but the keyword is *opportunity*. You have to consciously choose to work with these energies by seeing how you can incorporate them into your life. For example, a Venus/Neptune sextile would provide an opportunity to be really creative, imaginative, and romantic, but with a tendency to be a little submissive. Choosing to pursue the creative and romantic impulse instead of waiting for it to come to you would be beneficial.

TRINE △ −90°

ORBS: all planets generally up to 5°

The planets involved in a trine work together really well, but this harmonious aspect is probably the "laziest" in that the talents created by the aspect are natural to us, and we tend to take them for granted. Our conscious choice to make use of these energies is more necessary than with any other major aspect. For example, a Mercury/Mars trine indicates someone with a very quick mind who can excel at anything that requires active and fast thought, but because this is a trine, this comes so naturally to this person that they may neglect to actually use this energy to their advantage. Once this person is aware of this natural talent, they are more likely to use it.

Table of Aspects

PLANET IN THIS SIGN	LOOK FOR OPPOSITIONS IN:	LOOK FOR SQUARES IN:	LOOK FOR SEXTILES IN:	LOOK FOR TRINES IN:
Aries	Libra	Cancer, Capricorn	Gemini, Aquarius	Leo, Sagittarius
Taurus	Scorpio	Leo, Aquarius	Cancer, Pisces	Virgo, Capricorn
Gemini	Sagittarius	Virgo, Pisces	Leo, Aries	Libra, Aquarius
Cancer	Capricorn	Aries, Libra	Virgo, Taurus	Scorpio, Pisces
Leo	Aquarius	Taurus, Scorpio	Gemini, Libra	Aries, Sagittarius
Virgo	Pisces	Gemini, Sagittarius	Cancer, Scorpio	Taurus, Capricorn
Libra	Aries	Cancer, Capricorn	Leo, Sagittarius	Gemini, Aquarius
Scorpio	Taurus	Leo, Aquarius	Virgo, Capricorn	Cancer, Pisces
Sagittarius	Gemini	Virgo, Pisces	Libra, Aquarius	Aries, Leo
Capricorn	Cancer	Aries, Libra	Scorpio, Pisces	Taurus, Virgo
Aquarius	Leo	Taurus, Scorpio	Aries, Sagittarius	Gemini, Libra
Pisces	Virgo	Gemini, Sagittarius	Taurus, Capricorn	Cancer, Scorpio

IDENTIFYING ASPECTS

In your natal chart, you can identify your aspects by using a grid or the lines in the middle of the chart to figure out the angle. The more dynamic aspects usually appear in red and the harmonious in blue. They will usually have the symbol placed on the line. Some astrology-calculation software provides a grid. Which method works best is a matter of preference. I "see" the aspects more easily in the chart itself; for others, the grid or table works best.

Once you know how to identify your aspects, use your journal to list them and incorporate your collected keywords and phrases as you write your thoughts about how the energies work together within you. This is more beneficial than cookie-cutter definitions because it allows you to really feel the energies.

For example, if you have Mercury in Gemini in opposition to Saturn in Sagittarius in your chart, you can combine words for Mercury (mind), Gemini (perception, communication), Saturn (mastery, control), and Sagittarius (truth, freedom). You might feel that your free-ranging mind is sometimes restricted, but you actually have a fabulous opportunity to use the energies of the opposition for some highly concentrated study. You will also want to add in the house placements of the aspect. If, for example, the Sun is in the twelfth house and Saturn is in the sixth house, you blend words and phrases from your journaling about your Sun in the twelfth house and Saturn in the sixth house to give you coherent meaning in your life.

I encourage you to really take the time to feel how the energies manifest within you and for you to navigate them to your own advantage.

WORKING WITH TRANSITS

All astrology is based on the natal chart, which, as discussed, is the cosmic blueprint of your soul and personality at the time and place where you took your first breath. This blueprint carries you through your life and shows you your personality traits and your human potential. It's essential to have a deep understanding of your natal chart as a basis for all astrological pursuits because it is really a map for life.

This cosmic blueprint is not, however, a static description of an unchanging human being. I mentioned previously that it shows your potential, which can be achieved by using your free will to explore the meanings of the signs, planets, houses, and their relationships. Throughout your life, however, the universe is unfolding and the planets are moving, and each time a planet transits a point in your natal chart, it triggers an aspect of that point to encourage you to evolve.

Transits work in a similar way to aspects, except that they are transitional not permanent. Transits refer to the movement of the planets in relation to the fixed point in time of your birth. Transits are the main way to explore how the current and upcoming cosmic energies are affecting you personally. In Evolutionary Astrology, they are used to forecast periods of emotional and psychological challenge and growth.

As the planets move, they make transiting aspects to your natal planets with the slower-moving, "outer" planets (Jupiter through Pluto), creating a longer-lasting and more profound impact. Just as we blend the meanings of the planet, sign, and house in aspects, you will do the same with a transiting aspect to give yourself an idea of how that energy is or will be affecting you and your personal growth.

To do this, the transiting planets are laid out in a chart around the natal chart (see the sample chart with transits on page 215), and we look at the angles they make to the natal planets. Some astrological software does this for you, and some also provide "dynamic" reports with lists of transits. For example, if Pluto is at 21° Capricorn and your Sun is at 21° Capricorn, Pluto is transiting conjunct your natal Sun in Capricorn. Smaller orbs would be used than for natal aspects, usually 3° when the transiting planet is "applying," or moving toward the natal planet, or 2° when the transiting planet is "separating," or moving away from a planet.

I suggest getting to know your natal chart well before looking at transiting aspects. Take into consideration how you have lived your chart up to now and whether you wish to make different choices from now on. When you look at transits, it can be helpful to look back at major turning points in your life to understand how transits affected your personal growth so that you can use this information to understand how future transits will affect you.

Once you understand all of this fairly well, use that basis to choose how you face both harmonious and dynamic transits, always remembering that there is nothing broken or wrong; there is only awareness and choice. The aim is to learn to accept and love all of you—not to become an idealized perfect being, because there is no such thing. The aim is also to help you make choices with awareness and understanding rather than feeling as if you are at the whim of outer energies and forces.

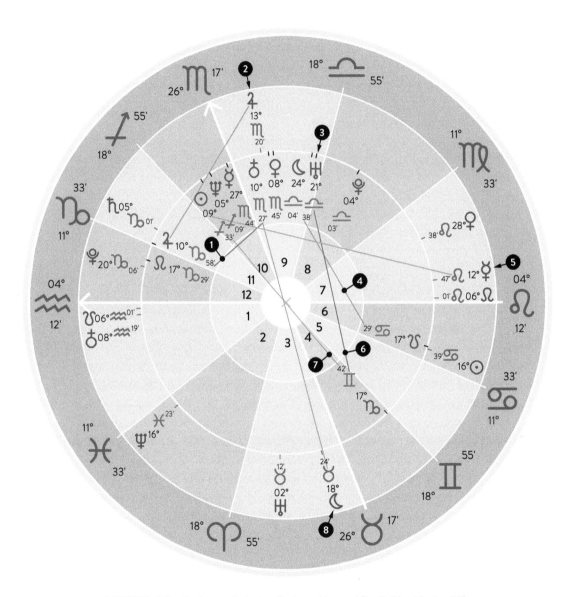

LEGEND: 1. Sextile Aspect; **2**. Jupiter Conjunct Mars and Sextile Natal Jupiter 57°;
3. Conjunction Aspect; **4**. Square Aspect 95°; **5**. Mercury Transit Trine Sun 87°;
6. Trine Aspect 94°; **7**. Opposition Aspect 188°; **8**. Moon Transit Opposition Mars 188°

TRANSITS IN ACTION

Transits by personal planets—the Sun, the Moon, Mercury, Venus, and Mars—are fast moving; they are generally used to plan the timing of events and to understand when you may have power days or days of rest. Because they are not often used for personal growth, we will look at the slowest-moving planets first.

- Take note of where Pluto, Neptune, Uranus, Saturn, and Jupiter are now by sign, house, and degree.
- Note if any of these have moved or are just about to move into a new house or sign. Make notes using the sections to describe the energies of that sign or house and blend those with words that describe the transiting planet.
- Note whether any of these transiting planets are making major aspects to your Sun, Moon, Mercury, Venus, Mars, Ascendant, or Midheaven. Again, blend keywords to help you understand how these transits are encouraging you to grow and evolve.

The influence of all of these planets will be felt before the transit is exact. A good guide is 3° before the transit is exact (this is called "applying") and 2° after (this is called "separating").

These outer planet transits often transit a point three or more times due to apparent retrograde motion, which extends the period of the transit's evolutionary impulse. The first exact pass is usually where the transformation begins or is planted. The middle pass is often a crisis point where any evolutionary stress is most felt, and the last pass is where the resolution comes or where you find the path forward.

There are more computations of transits than could possibly be outlined in this book, so going back and first getting to know the energies in your natal chart is of primary importance. Then you will be more able to understand the energies involved.

PLUTO: death and rebirth (figuratively), transformation, transmutation
NEPTUNE: dissolving, spiritualizing, confusion, idealism
URANUS: awakening, sudden change, aha moments, reinvention, restlessness
SATURN: mastery, maturity, time slowing down, things feeling hard and difficult
JUPITER: expansion, movement

Here are some brief examples:

- Pluto transiting the Sun can bring transformation of the ego and self, helping you step more into the power of who you truly are at your core. Pluto enables you to throw off external conditioning.
- Uranus transiting the cusp of the fourth house could mean a sudden change of home circumstances or an inner awakening that leads to a more fulfilling inner life.
- Saturn transiting the first house can be a great period of maturation in how you show up in the world.

Transits help you grow and evolve over your lifetime. They bring both inner and outer transformation. It's helpful to not look at transits as good or bad because each one has both possibilities, and your free will regarding how you respond and react to transits will reflect how much you choose to evolve through these planetary cycles.

CONCLUSION

Astrology is a deep and broad subject that astrologers spend decades learning in depth. I encourage you to not allow this to overwhelm you. Great insights and growth can be found by keeping things fairly simple and mastering the basics before being tempted to go deeper. There is a lot to take in, and you can't possibly do so just by reading this book once and setting it aside. Here are my suggestions for you to continue to make the most of this book for your own personal growth.

First, breathe and slow down. Then go back to the beginning. I liken astrology to the rabbit hole in *Alice in Wonderland.* It's a journey of exploration that takes unexpected twists and turns where you learn something more at every turn and with each new event. Repetition is important to begin integrating the meanings of the energies into your awareness.

I encourage you to do more shamanic journey work and continue journaling so that you *feel* the energies of the signs, planets, and houses rather than thinking about them as an intellectual exercise. Remember, all of the energies are contained within you; they are not merely "out there." You are a microcosm of the universe, and my aim is for you to gain a deep level of understanding of all you are so that you can use that awareness to choose how you are in the world and how you respond and react to the world.

Always remember that there is nothing good or bad within you. You are created perfectly. You have free will with regard to how you work with the cosmic blueprint you chose in this lifetime. Evolutionary Astrology can bring great peace to the soul as you accept that you can only work with what you have rather than trying to become someone you are not.

I encourage you to practice the exercises over and over. As you do, you will deepen your self-love and self-acceptance. Evolutionary growth is a process. It is not something you can achieve and then you are changed for life. So again, breathe, slow down, and begin a process that will transform your life for the better.

blending the chart (case study)

This case study explores how to blend the parts of the chart so that you can do the same for your own natal chart. I will break down some sections of the chart piece by piece and then offer a short integrated analysis. Refer to the sample chart from chapter 1, included again here, for this case study.

KEY PLACEMENTS

In this section, we'll focus on the key placements in the sample chart. I will show you examples of how the energies can be blended to create a coherent and integrated description of how the energies work within you.

SUN IN SAGITTARIUS IN THE TENTH HOUSE

The Sun is the core or ego. Sagittarius represents freedom-seeking, and, in the tenth house, it signals that this person may have different public roles in another person's life and even have more than one at a time because they love variety. These roles may involve travel, writing, teaching, and/or working with foreign cultures. The Sun in the tenth house indicates that the person is very attached to their career or mission in life.

MOON IN LIBRA IN THE NINTH HOUSE

The Moon rules emotions, and with Libra in the ninth house, this person is drawn to enjoy learning about belief systems and other cultures and has a very strong sense of fairness and justice philosophically. They are, therefore, emotionally connected to these issues.

AQUARIUS ASCENDANT

This person is seen as rebellious and unique. They help others to see how things need to be changed and can show them what a different future could look like. More than anything, they want to be seen as different and may dress accordingly, maintaining a different and unique look. Others will be drawn to them to help solve problems and create innovative solutions.

INTEGRATING THE CHART

The Sun, Moon, and Ascendant are the primary elements of your personality in your natal chart. When we put these three elements together in this case study, we have someone who is likely to be concerned with humanitarianism, equality, and freedom. The mix of Fire (Sagittarius) and Air (Libra and Aquarius) means that they have a lot of energy and are likely to be outgoing and concerned with their public impact in the world (the tenth house, or Midheaven).

After considering these primary elements, there is no one right way to look at the rest. We can go through each planet one by one, taking the keywords and phrases we have collected and blending them by planet, sign, and house, or we might choose to look at aspects first and then start blending to create a complete picture. For example, Mercury in Scorpio conjunct (meaning, in conjunction with) the cusp of the tenth house, or Midheaven, indicates that this person has a powerfully transformative (Scorpio) voice and message (Mercury), while Neptune conjunct the Sun in Sagittarius might make that voice about philosophical and spiritual beliefs. The opposition from the Sun to Saturn (mastery, leadership) in Gemini (voice, perception) in the fourth house (nature of inner life) adds gravitas to that message.

Next, we turn to the four planets that are in the ninth house, the natural house of Sagittarius. Four planets in this house alone add to the story of this person: they are outgoing and concerned with freedom, truth, and philosophical matters.

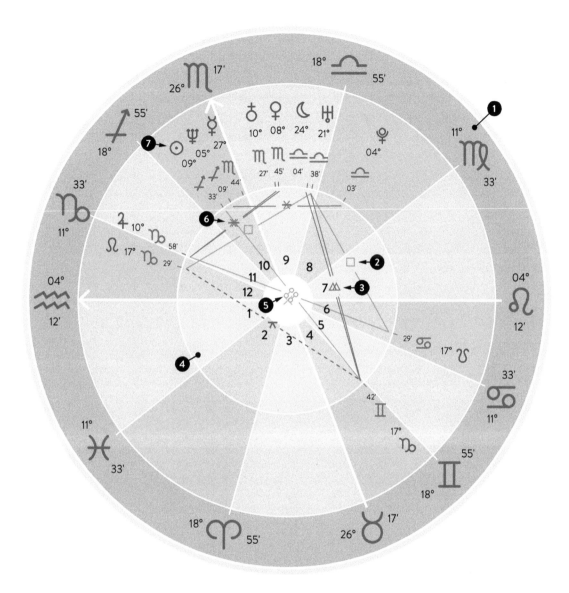

LEGEND: **1**. Signs; **2**. Square Aspect; **3**. Trine Aspect; **4**. Houses by number, counterclockwise; **5**. Opposition Aspect; **6**. Sextile Aspect; **7**. Planets

Next, we look at the energies there. First that Libra Moon, which is concerned with equality and justice, is conjunct the ruler of the Ascendant, Uranus, giving a more radical feel to these concerns. The Moon/Uranus conjunction is squared to the Moon's Nodes, which means that this person may have difficulty integrating these radical feelings in a way that helps them strive toward the evolutionary potential of their North Node in Capricorn (goal-oriented, problem-solving) in the twelfth house (focus on trust, surrender, and compassion rather than control: South Node in Virgo).

Venus (feminine principle) and Mars (male principle) and conjunct in Scorpio in the ninth house add another layer to the theme of equality in this chart. In Scorpio, this person may focus their powerful message (Mercury/Midheaven in Scorpio) on themes of sexual inequality and abuse of power. These two planets are aspecting Jupiter (ruler of the Sagittarius Sun), who is widely (has a wide orb) conjunct the Capricorn North Node, meaning this person has the ability to become a truth guide and leader if they can soften their own radical and erratic emotions (Moon/Uranus in Libra).

Last but not least, their soul's desire, Pluto, is in the house that is naturally ruled by Pluto and Scorpio, the eighth house. This indicates someone with the potential to completely transform other people's lives and one who might be a therapist or energy healer.

When we put all this together, we can pick out strong themes of healing (Scorpio Midheaven and Pluto in the eighth house), belief, truth, and teaching (Sagittarius and the ninth house), equality (Libra Moon and Venus/Mars), and humanitarianism (Aquarius and Uranus conjunct the Moon), and mastery and leadership (Capricorn in the twelfth house); Mercury conjunct the Midheaven emphasizes the teaching energy.

Using the themes identified, this person can conclude that they might make a strong therapist or healer of some kind—especially one who uses their higher mind and their interest in belief and truth to teach others to find their way forward in life. Their strong, emotionally detached energy may bring them issues as others may find them distant and think they are "in their head" a lot. Focusing on grounding that energy and bringing more emotional connection through grounding and heart-opening meditations or spending time in nature will help them be more connected to the world.

All charts have themes woven throughout them, and finding your own themes by blending your own collection of keywords and phrases for each sign, planet, and house will enable you to discover deep knowledge about yourself. When you start to see a cohesive picture, you will begin to find deep acceptance of yourself and start making choices that align with your strengths.

keywords and themes for planets and signs

In this appendix, you will find suggested keywords and themes for the planets and signs. Please keep in mind that they are only suggestions. I want you to use words and phrases that resonate for you. My suggestion is that you use this section and the information in the book to create your own lists in your journal for each planet and sign. This will not only help you integrate the learning of the energies but will also make them more meaningful to you. That's how you will learn to understand at a deeper level.

AQUARIUS: personal freedom, loyalty to truth, unpredictable, original, inventive, contrary, questions authority, fanatical, future-oriented, anarchistic, socially conscious, emotionally distant, humanitarian, honors diversity, friendship as core value

ARIES: pioneering, aggressive, initiating, angry, independent, impulsive, energizing, reactionary, inspirational, volatile, direct, quick, competitive, healthy self-interest, "me first," risk-taking, impatient, entrepreneurial

CANCER: nurturing, insecure, sensitive, hypersensitive, responsive, moody, feeling, overprotective, emotionally connective, introverted, sentimental, intuitive/instinctive, domestic, family oriented, loves tradition, clings to past

CAPRICORN: responsible, authoritarian, disciplined, controlling, committed, fearful, determined, practical, hardworking, judgmental, leader, hidden insecurities, achievement, workaholic, law-abiding, engenders respect, connected to physical realm

GEMINI: verbally expressive, socially adept, mentally active, talks a lot, curious, questioning, duplicitous, adaptable, scattered, avid learner, inconsistent, perceptive, nosy, observant, gossip, witty, high-strung, networker

JUPITER: expansion, breadth, religion, philosophy, faith, belief, truth, freedom, ethics, joy, humor, optimism, generosity, luck, grandiosity, inflation

LEO: dynamic, self-confident, demands attention, natural leader, arrogant, generous, grandiose, playful, charming, dramatic, shine, perform, melodramatic

LIBRA: relationship focus, other-oriented, codependent, diplomatic, peace at any price, sees both sides, vacillating, fairness, indecisive, social justice-oriented, focused on appearances, cooperative, considerate, finds it hard to say no, mediating, contradictory, negotiator, contrary, argumentative, balance, pacifying, devil's advocate, the arts

♂ **MARS:** yang/masculine energy, action, drive, will, courage, work, sexuality, physicality, assertion, aggression, anger, fighting, competitive, war

MERCURY: intelligence, perception, mind, voice, communication, writing, listening, learning style

☽ **MOON:** emotional body, basis of security, needs, feelings, body rhythms, source of nurture and comfort, response to stress, mother/women, family/home, the past, powerful femininity

NEPTUNE: consciousness, altered states, psychic sensitivity, creative energy, mysticism, mystery, dreams, healing, sacrifice, lack of boundaries, confusion, illusion, delusion, addiction, victimization

NORTH NODE: new evolutionary direction, soul guidance, unfamiliarity, karmic lessons, midlife shift

PISCES: spiritual, addictive tendencies, compassionate, hypersensitive, intuitive, lack of boundaries, sensitive, victim/martyr, creative, mystic, rescuer/savior, mediumistic, hermit, humanitarian, healing

PLUTO: personal transformation, psychological depth, intensity, power, underlying reality, karmic wound, sexuality, taboo, fate, soul, repression, survival, obsession

SAGITTARIUS: truth seeker, experience-driven, faith and belief as motivator, spiritually oriented, freedom-loving, self-determined, optimist, independent, inspirational, visionary, big-picture seer, explorer, wanderer, wonderer

SATURN: external authority, parent, father, boundaries, mastery, rules, limitation, discipline, maturity, tradition, fear, denial, control

SCORPIO: emotionally deep and complex, secretive, innately psychological, obsessive, instinctive, focused on negative, comfortable with taboo issues, cruel, private, abusive, powerful, revengeful, magnetic, intimidating, good in crises, overpowering, brooding, survivor

SOUTH NODE: soul marker, soul habit (deeply ingrained), theme across lifetimes, innate abilities, default setting

SUN: core, vitality, identity, ego, self-expression, purpose, leadership

TAURUS: natural builder, embodies animal wisdom, territorial, grounded, stubborn, patient, resists change, practical, possessive, persevering, materialistic, loyal, affectionate, sensual, obsessed with material security, body-focused, nature lover, preserver, lacks pretense

URANUS: individuality, personal truth, independence, unconventionality, difference/uniqueness, sudden change, erratic, unpredictable, genius, reform, revolution, rebellion

VENUS: yin/female energy, relating, beauty, love, attraction, values, desire, sensuality, taste, style, the arts, creativity

VIRGO: service mind-set, detail oriented, analytical, modest, servant mentality, hand skills/talents, perfectionist, efficient, critical, organized, self-critical, technical and editorial abilities, detail obsessed, health-conscious, self-effacing, ethical, worrier, economical

glossary of terms

AIR SIGNS: Zodiac signs that correspond to the element Air—Gemini, Libra, and Aquarius.

ANGLES: Ascendant (ASC), Descendant (DSC), Midheaven (MC), and Nadir or Imum Coeli (IC). These refer to the cusps of the first, seventh, tenth, and fourth houses, respectively.

ASCENDANT (ASC): The cusp of the first house, also known as the rising sign; the point that is rising on the eastern horizon at the moment and place of birth.

ASPECTS: Angular relationships between points in the natal chart.

CARDINAL SIGNS: Zodiac signs that correspond to the cardinal quality—Aries, Cancer, Libra, and Capricorn.

CUSP: In the natal chart, the beginning of a house or where one sign ends and another begins.

DESCENDANT (DSC): Cusp of the seventh house in the natal chart, directly opposite the Ascendant.

EARTH SIGNS: Zodiac signs that correspond to the element Earth—Taurus, Virgo, and Capricorn.

ELEMENTS: Fire, Earth, Air, and Water.

FIRE SIGNS: Zodiac signs that correspond to the element Fire—Aries, Leo, and Sagittarius.

FIXED SIGNS: Zodiac signs that correspond to the fixed quality—Taurus, Leo, Scorpio, and Aquarius.

GLYPHS: Symbols used for the astrological signs, planets, luminaries, and aspects.

HOUSES: The 12 segments of the natal chart; each house rules over a different area of life.

LUMINARIES: The Sun and Moon (in this book, they are grouped under the term "planets").

MIDHEAVEN (MC): The cusp of the tenth house of the natal chart, the highest point in the zodiac at moment of birth, and the most public area of the chart.

MUTABLE SIGNS: Zodiac signs that correspond to the mutable quality—Gemini, Virgo, Sagittarius, and Pisces.

ORB: Number of degrees from exact between aspect degrees.

PLANETARY RULERS: The planets that rule each sign.

SATURN RETURN: The time when Saturn returns to the point it was in the natal chart; it has done a full cycle through the zodiac. All planets have "returns," but Saturn is one of the most profound and best known; it occurs around the ages of 29, 58, and 87.

SHAMANISM: A spiritual practice in which an individual enters an altered state of consciousness to interact with the spirit/unconscious realms.

STELLIUM: Three or more zodiac signs in one house.

WATER SIGNS: Zodiac signs that correspond to the element Water—Cancer, Scorpio, and Pisces.

glossary of symbols and glyphs

 Aquarius

 Leo

 North Node

 South Node

 Aries

 Libra

 Pisces

 Sun

 Cancer

 Mars

Pluto

Taurus

 Capricorn

Mercury

Sagittarius

Uranus

Gemini

Moon

Saturn

Venus

 Jupiter

Neptune

Scorpio

Virgo

further reading

If you would like to continue your journey into astrology, these are books that I recommend. They are all written by leading Evolutionary Astrologers and will deepen your knowledge and understanding. I chose these titles because I have found them to be the most helpful in my own astrology practice.

Forrest, Steven. *The Changing Sky: Learning Predictive Astrology.* 2nd ed. Borrego Springs, CA: Seven Paws Press, 2008.

Forrest, Steven. *The Inner Sky: How to Make Wiser Choices for a More Fulfilling Life.* Reprint ed. Borrego Springs, CA: Seven Paws Press, 2007.

Green, Jeff. *Pluto: The Evolutionary Journey of the Soul, Volumes 1 and 2.* 2nd rev. ed. Swanage, UK: The Wessex Astrologer Ltd., 2011.

Jones, Mark. *Healing the Soul: Pluto, Uranus, and the Lunar Nodes.* Portland, OR: Raven Dreams Press, 2011.

Spiller, Jan. *Astrology for the Soul.* New York: Bantam, 1997.

references

Andrews, Ted. *Animal Speak: The Spiritual and Magical Powers of Creatures Great and Small.* Woodbury, MN: Llewellyn Publications, 2002.

Astrology Club. "Astrology Club Homepage." Accessed July 3, 2018. astrologyclub.org.

Café Astrology. "Café Astrology Homepage." Accessed July 3, 2018. cafeastrology.com.

Cameron, Julia. *The Artist's Way.* Anniversary ed. New York, NY: TarcherPerigee, 2016.

Forrest, Steven. *The Inner Sky: How to Make Wiser Choices for a More Fulfilling Life.* Reprint ed. Borrego Springs, CA: Seven Paws Press, 2007.

Ingerman, Sandra. *Shamanic Journeying: A Beginner's Guide.* Louisville, CO: Sounds True, 2008.

ThoughtCo. "Astrology." Accessed July 3, 2018. www.thoughtco.com/astrology -4133112.

index

about the author

LOUISE EDINGTON has been studying and practicing astrology as an interest for 30 years and working professionally as an Evolutionary Astrologer since 2012. Louise has also been writing daily astrology posts since 2012 on Facebook, and now on Medium and Patreon. She enjoys all aspects of professional astrology, but her main passion is helping clients understand how the energies work within them so that they can live a fulfilled life characterized by deep understanding and acceptance of who they truly are. She does this through providing astrological counseling, teaching astrology classes, and writing. You can learn more about her services at louiseedington.com, and also follow Louise on patreon.com/louiseedington, medium .com/@louiseedington, and facebook.com /WildWomanUnleashed.

CPSIA information can be obtained
at www.ICGtesting.com
Printed in the USA
VHW01s2150101018
)2985LV00001B/1/P

9 781641 522267